ENGLISH FOR TODAY'S WORLD

JOAN SASLOW
ALLEN ASCHER

With *Top Notch Pop* Songs and Karaoke
by Rob Morsberger

Top Notch: English for Today's World   Fundamentals B, Third Edition

Copyright © 2015 by Pearson Education, Inc.
All rights reserved. No part of this publication may be reproduced, stored in a retrieval system, or transmitted in any form or by any means, electronic, mechanical, photocopying, recording, or otherwise, without the prior permission of the publisher.

Pearson Education, 10 Bank Street, White Plains, NY 10606 USA

Staff credits: The people who made up the *Top Notch* team are Peter Benson, Kimberly Casey, Jennifer Castro, Tracey Munz Cataldo, Rosa Chapinal, Aerin Csigay, Dave Dickey, Gina DiLillo, Nancy Flaggman, Irene Frankel, Shelley Gazes, Christopher Leonowicz, Julie Molnar, Laurie Neaman, Sherri Pemberton, Pamela Pia, Rebecca Pitke, Jennifer Raspiller, Charlene Straub, and Kenneth Volcjak.

Cover photo: Sprint/Corbis
Text composition: TSI Graphics

Library of Congress Cataloging-in-Publication Data

Saslow, Joan M.
  Top Notch : English for today's world. Fundamentals / Joan Saslow, Allen Ascher ; With Top Notch Pop Songs
    and Karaoke by Rob Morsberger. — Third Edition.
        pages cm
  Includes biographical references.
  ISBN 978-0-13-354275-2 — ISBN 978-0-13-339348-4 — ISBN 978-0-13-354277-6 — ISBN 978-0-13-354278-3   1. English language
    — Textbooks for foreign speakers. 2. English language—Problems, exercises, etc. 3. English language — Sound recordings for foreign
    speakers. I. Ascher, Allen. II. Morsberger, Robert Eustis, 1929- III. Title. IV. Title: English for today's world.
  PE1128.S2757 2015
  428.2'4 — dc23
                            2013044020

Printed in the United States of America
ISBN-10:   0-13-392776-8
ISBN-13: 978-0-13-392776-4
1 2 3 4 5 6 7 8 9 10—V003—19 18 17 16 15 14

pearsonelt.com/topnotch3e

In Memoriam

Rob Morsberger (1959–2013)

The authors wish to acknowledge their memory of and gratitude to **Rob Morsberger**, the gifted composer and songwriter of the *Top Notch Pop* Songs and Karaoke that have provided learners both language practice and pleasure.

Photo credits: Original photography by Sharon Hoogstraten and David Mager. Page 65 (1) Javier Larrea/AGE Fotostock, (2) Dmitry Pistrov /Fotolia, (3) Frank Boston/Fotolia, (4) Ed Brennan/Fotolia, (5) Janine Wiedel Photolibrary/Alamy, (6) Robert Harding World Imagery/Alamy, (7) Shutterbas/Fotolia, (8) Spotmatikphoto/Fotolia; p. 67 (top left) Bartok007/Fotolia, (top right) MasterLu/Fotolia; p. 69 (red chair) Amadorgs/Fotolia, (mirror) Anna Biancoloto/Shutterstock, (brown lamp) Zerbor/Fotolia, (mat) Africa Studio/Fotolia, (household) Mrgarry/Fotolia; p. 70 (bg) Artur Bogacki /Fotolia, (left) Imtmphoto/Fotolia, (middle) Bevangoldswain/Fotolia, (right) Antonio Nunes/Fotolia; p. 75 Tetra Images/AGE Fotostock; p. 77 Maridav/Fotolia; p. 81 (green bean salad) Marco Mayer/Fotolia, (Fruit salad) Matthias Krapp/Shutterstock, (tomato potato soup) Robert6666/Fotolia, (potato pancake) Kolazig/Fotolia, (stuffed peppers) M.studio/Fotolia; p. 92 (1) Haveseen/Fotolia, (2) Rido/Fotolia, (3) Purestock/Getty Images, (4) Michael Jung/Fotolia, (5) Claro Alindogan/iStock/Thinkstock/Getty Images, (6) Bikeriderlondon/Shutterstock; p. 94 (top left) Fotoluminate LLC/Fotolia, (middle left) Szefei/iStock/Thinkstock/Getty Images, (bottom left) Nyul/Fotolia, (bottom right) Nejron Photo/Shutterstock; p. 96 (1) Creativa/Fotolia, (2) Sanneberg/Fotolia, (3) Alinute/Fotolia, (4) Goodluz/Fotolia, (5) Digitalefotografien/Fotolia, (6) Contrastwerkstatt/Fotolia, (9) BigLike Images/Fotolia, (10) Auremar/Fotolia, (12) Zea Lenanet/Fotolia, (13) Eurobanks/Fotolia, (top right) Jose Manuel Gelpi Diaz/Hemera/Thinkstock/Getty Images, (bottom left) Jeanette Dietl/Fotolia, (3a) Siri Stafford/Photodisc/Getty Images, (3c) 2/Mel Curtis/Ocean/Corbis, (3d) Peter Atkins/Fotolia; z) Andrea Comas/Reuters/Newscom, (Bocelli) Allen Berezovsky/WireImage/Getty Images, (Adams) Derek Ross/LFI/Photoshot/Newscom, (Sandé) Infusny-261/AlbertoReyes/INFphoto.com/Newscom, (Hemsworth) BT1 WENN Photos/Newscom; p. 98 (12, 13, 14) Christian Schwier/Fotolia, (15, 16, 17) Vibe Images/Fotolia; p. 100 (1) JupiterImages/Pixland/Thinkstock/Getty Images, (2) Nyul/Fotolia, (3) Mirkoni/Shutterstock, (4 see a doctor) WaveBreakMediaMicro/Fotolia, (4 see a dentist) DragonImages/Fotolia; p. 102 (top left) Baverel-Lefranc/Kipa/Corbis, (middle left) ZUMA Press, Inc./Alamy, (top right) Cortesia Notimex/Newscom, (middle right) Jean Catuffe, PacificCoastNews/Newscom; p. 105 (top left) Edyta Pawlowska/Fotolia, (top right) Studio-Annika/iStock/Thinkstock/Getty Images; p. 107 (middle right) Cusp/SuperStock, (lunch) Igor Mojzes/Fotolia, (walk) Michael Jung/Fotolia, (cycling) Purestock/Getty Images, (driving) Bikeriderlondon/Shutterstock; p. 113 (1) John Neubauer/PhotoEdit, Inc., (2) Uwimages/Fotolia, (3) Michael Jung/Fotolia, (4) Apops/Fotolia, (5) Igor Mojzes/Fotolia, (6) Mitarart/Fotolia, (7) Andres Rodriguez/Fotolia, (8) Michael Jung/Fotolia, (9) Michael Jung/Fotolia, (10) APG/Alamy, (bottom right) Stuart Jenner/Shutterstock; p. 115 (top right) Arek_malang/Shutterstock, (driving) Bikeriderlondon/Shutterstock, (cleaning) Justinb/Fotolia, (Angler) Sabine Naumann/Fotolia, (watching TV) Brian Jackson/Fotolia, (relaxing) Shutterstock; p. 116 (1) Paylessimages/Fotolia, (2) Tyler Olson/Fotolia, (3) Cohen/Ostrow/Photodisc/Getty Images, (4a) Duckman76/Fotolia, (4b) Duckman76/Fotolia, (5) Mc Xas/Fotolia, (6) Ryanking999/Fotolia, (7) Feng Yu/Shutterstock, (8) Claudia Paulussen/Fotolia; p. 118 (left) GL Archive/Alamy, (right) Ray Roberts/ Alamy; p. 119 (Miranda Lewis) Todd Keith/iStock/Thinkstock/Getty Images, (Miranda's house) Blend Images–JGI/Brand X Pictures/Getty Images, (Millerton State Business College) Andres Rodriguez/Fotolia, (Miranda today) Andres Rodriguez/Fotolia; p. 120 (3a) Dmitry Pistrov/Fotolia, (3b) Qingwa/Fotolia, (4a) Paolo Bona/AGE Fotostock, (4b) Shutterbas/Fotolia, (5a) CandyBox Images/Fotolia, (5b) Uwimages/Fotolia; p. 121 (right) WaveBreakMediaMicro/Fotolia; p. 123 (1) Robert Kneschke/Shutterstock, (2) Auremar/Shutterstock, (3) Jack Hollingsworth/Blend Images/Thinkstock/Getty Images, (4) Eurobanks/Shutterstock, (5) Ingram Publishing/Thinkstock/Getty Images, (6) Cameron Whitman/iStock/Thinkstock/Getty Images, (7) Francisco Romero/E+/Getty Images, (bottom right) JupiterImages/Stockbyte/Thinkstock/Getty Images; p. 129 (1,2,3) RSnapshotPhotos/Shutterstock, (4) Red Chopsticks/Getty Images, (5) Cbckchristine/Fotolia, (6) Ignatius Wooster/Fotolia, (7,8,9) Celiafoto/Fotolia, (10,11) Zoonar GmbH / Alamy, (12) Ilya Akinshin/Fotolia, (13) Tiler84/Fotolia, (14) Don Farrall/Getty Images,(15,16) Alexandr79/Fotolia, (17,18) Roman Samokhin/Fotolia, (19) Piotr Pawinski/Fotolia, (20) MP2/Fotolia, (21,22) Womue/Fotolia, (23) Bonchan/Shutterstock, (24) Bruce Shippee/Fotolia, (25) Aleksandr Ugorenkov/Fotolia,(26) Andrey Kuzmin/Fotolia, (27,28,29,30) Kornienko/Fotolia, (31,32,33,34) Food Collection/Getty Images, (35) 3dmentat/Fotolia, (36) HSN/Fotolia; p. 130 (top) (1) Soniccc/Fotolia, (2) Dianis Derics/Shutterstock, (3) Danita Delimont/Alamy, (4) James Thew/Fotolia, (bottom) (1,2,3,4) Dennis MacDonald/Alamy; p. 131 (top) (1,2,3,8,9,10) Cynoclub/Fotolia, (4,5,6) Serghei Velusceac/Fotolia, (7) Ric Esplana Babor/Fotolia, (11) Mates/Fotolia, (12) Giuseppe Porzani/Fotolia, (13) Denlo109/Fotolia,(14) Fotomatrix/Fotolia, (15) Pieropoma/Fotolia,(bottom 1,2) Arti Zav/Fotolia, (3,4,5,14) Vinicius Tupinamba/Fotolia, (6) Volf/Fotolia, (7) Natika/Fotolia, (8,9,10,11,12,13) Giuseppe Porzani/Fotolia,(15) Strannik72/Shutterstock, (16) Orlorl/Fotolia, (17,18) Popova Olga/Fotolia ; p. 132 (1) George Dolgikh/Fotolia, (2) Zvonimir Ore /Shutterstock, (3) Miravision/Fotolia, (4) Alexey Fursov /Shutterstock, (5) BlueOrange Studio /Shutterstock, (6) Vixit /Shutterstock, (7) Lightpoet/Fotolia, (8) Dima266f/Fotolia, (face) Jaimie Duplass/Fotolia, (body) Edyta Pawlowska/Fotolia, (tongue) ArenaCreative/Fotolia; p. 133 (1) Sbarabu/Fotolia, (2) Scalaphotography/Fotolia, (3) MUE/Fotolia, (4) Bota Horatiu/Fotolia, (5) Seen/Fotolia, (6) Klaus Eppele/Fotolia, (7) Eyetronic/Fotolia, (8) Dmitry Vereshchagin/Fotolia, (9) Jules Selmes/Dorling Kindersley, Ltd., (10) Dispicture/Fotolia, (11) Klaus Eppele/Fotolia, (12) ReMuS/Fotolia; p. 134 (1) Dougal Waters/Getty Images, (2) Hill Street Studios/AGE Fotostock, (3) Radu Razvan/Fotolia, (4) WavebreakMediaMicro/Fotolia, (5) BostjanT/E+/Getty Images, (6) Redsnapper/Alamy, (skiing) ARochau/Fotolia, (hiking) Maygutyak/Fotolia, (play) Mat Hayward/Fotolia, (garden) Kazoka303030/Fotolia, (curise) Frank Boston/Fotolia, (manicure) Mariiya/Fotolia; p. 144 (dress) Demidoff/Fotolia, (long skirt) PhotosIndia.com LLC/Alamy; p. 145 (suit) Elnur/Fotolia.

Illustration credits: Kenneth Batelman pp. 64, 65, 66, 120; John Ceballos p. 95; Pascal Dejong p. 87; Karen Donnelly p. 111; Len Ebert p. 110; Scott Fray pp. 80, 83; Brian Hughes pp. 89, 92; Adam Larkum p. 103; Mona Mark p. 86; Robert McPhillips p. 119; Sandy Nichols p. 77; Dusan Petricic pp. 72, 98, 100, 112; Phil Scheuer pp. 98, 99, 104 (top, top right), 106; Gary Torrisi p. 68; Meryl Treatner pp. 110, 114; Anna Velfort pp. 76, 104, 106 (1-3 bottom); 108, 120 (bottom), 122; Patrick Welsh p. 71.

Text credit: Page 86: Recipe for "Hungarian Cabbage and Noodles" by Rozanne Gold. Reprinted by permission.

LEARNING OBJECTIVES

Top Notch Fundamentals is designed for true beginning students or for students needing the support of a very low-level beginning course. No prior knowledge of English is assumed or necessary.

	COMMUNICATION GOALS	VOCABULARY	GRAMMAR

UNIT 1
Names and Occupations
PAGE 4
	• Tell a classmate your occupation
	• Identify your classmates
	• Spell names
		• Occupations
		• The alphabet
		VOCABULARY BOOSTER
		• More occupations
			• Verb be:
			  ○ Singular and plural statements, contractions
			  ○ Yes / no questions and short answers
			  ○ Common errors
			• Subject pronouns
			• Articles a / an
			• Nouns:
			  ○ Singular and plural / Common and proper
			GRAMMAR BOOSTER Extra practice

UNIT 2 **About People** PAGE 12	• Introduce people • Tell someone your first and last name • Get someone's contact information	• Relationships (non-family) • Titles • First and last names • Numbers 0–20 VOCABULARY BOOSTER • More relationships / More titles	• Possessive nouns and adjectives • Be from / Questions with Where, common errors • Verb be: information questions with What GRAMMAR BOOSTER Extra practice
UNIT 3 **Places and How to Get There** PAGE 20	• Talk about locations • Discuss how to get places • Discuss transportation	• Places in the neighborhood • Locations • Ways to get places • Means of transportation • Destinations VOCABULARY BOOSTER • More places	• Verb be: questions with Where • Subject pronoun it • The imperative • By to express means of transportation GRAMMAR BOOSTER Extra practice

UNIT 4
Family
PAGE 28
	• Identify people in your family
	• Describe your relatives
	• Talk about your family
		• Family relationships
		• Adjectives to describe people
		• Numbers 21–101
		VOCABULARY BOOSTER
		• More adjectives
			• Verb be:
			  ○ Questions with Who and common errors
			  ○ With adjectives
			  ○ Questions with How old
			• Adverbs very and so
			• Verb have / has: affirmative statements
			GRAMMAR BOOSTER Extra practice

UNIT 5 **Events and Times** PAGE 36	• Confirm that you're on time • Talk about the time of an event • Ask about birthdays	• What time is it? • Early, on time, late • Events • Days of the week • Ordinal numbers • Months of the year VOCABULARY BOOSTER • More events	• Verb be: questions about time • Prepositions in, on, and at for dates and times • Contractions and common errors GRAMMAR BOOSTER Extra practice

UNIT 6
Clothes
PAGE 44
	• Give and accept a compliment
	• Ask for colors and sizes
	• Describe clothes
		• Clothes
		• Colors and sizes
		• Opposite adjectives to describe clothes
		VOCABULARY BOOSTER
		• More clothes
			• Demonstratives this, that, these, those
			• The simple present tense: like, want, need, and have:
			  ○ Affirmative and negative statements
			  ○ Questions and short answers
			  ○ Spelling rules and contractions
			• Adjective placement and common errors
			• One and ones
			GRAMMAR BOOSTER Extra practice

UNIT 7
Activities
PAGE 52
 	
Units 1–7 Review
PAGE 60
	• Talk about morning and evening activities
	• Describe what you do in your free time
	• Discuss household chores
		• Daily activities at home
		• Leisure activities
		• Household chores
		VOCABULARY BOOSTER
		• More household chores
			• The simple present tense:
			  ○ Third-person singular spelling rules
			  ○ Questions with When and What time
			  ○ Questions with How often, time expressions
			  ○ Questions with Who as subject, common errors
			• Frequency adverbs and time expressions:
			  ○ Usage, placement, and common errors
			GRAMMAR BOOSTER Extra practice

CONVERSATION STRATEGIES	LISTENING / PRONUNCIATION	READING / WRITING
• Use And you? to show interest in another person • Use Excuse me to initiate a conversation • Use Excuse me? to indicate you haven't heard or didn't understand • Use Thanks! to acknowledge someone's complying with a request	**Listening Tasks** • Circle the letter you hear • Identify correct spelling of names • Write the name you hear spelled • Identify the correct occupation • Write the missing information: names and occupations **Pronunciation** • Syllables	**Reading Text** • Simple forms and business cards **Writing Task** • Write affirmative and negative statements about people in a picture **WRITING BOOSTER** Guided writing practice
• Identify someone's relationship to you when making an introduction • Use too to reciprocate a greeting • Begin a question with And to indicate you want additional information • Repeat part of a question to clarify • Repeat information to confirm	**Listening Tasks** • Complete statements about relationships • Circle the correct information • Fill in names, phone numbers, and e-mail addresses you hear **Pronunciation** • Stress in two-word pairs	**Reading Text** • Short descriptions of famous people, their occupations, and countries of origin **Writing Task** • Write sentences about your relationships **WRITING BOOSTER** Guided writing practice
• Use You're welcome to formally acknowledge thanks • Use OK to acknowledge advice • Use What about you? to show interest in another person	**Listening Tasks** • Write the places you hear • Write the directions you hear, using affirmative and negative imperatives • Circle the means of transportation • Write by phrases, check destinations you hear **Pronunciation** • Falling intonation for questions with Where	**Reading Texts** • Simple maps and diagrams • Introductions of people, their relationships and occupations, where they live, and how they get to work **Writing Task** • Write questions and answers about the places in a complex picture **WRITING BOOSTER** Guided writing practice
• Use And to shift the topic • Use Tell me about to invite someone to talk about a topic • Use Well, to indicate you are deciding how to begin a response • Use And how about? to ask for more information • Use Really? to show interest or mild surprise	**Listening Tasks** • Identify the picture of a relative being described • Choose the adjective that describes the people mentioned in a conversation **Pronunciation** • Number contrasts	**Reading Texts** • A family tree • A magazine article about famous actors and their families **Writing Task** • Write a description of the people in your family **WRITING BOOSTER** Guided writing practice
• Use Uh-oh to indicate you may have made a mistake • Use Look to focus someone's attention on something • Use Great! to show enthusiasm for an idea • Offer someone best wishes on his or her birthday • Respond to a person's birthday wishes	**Listening Tasks** • Identify events and circle the correct times • Write the events you hear in a date book • Circle the dates you hear **Pronunciation** • Sentence rhythm	**Reading Texts** • A world map with time zones • Events posters • Newspaper announcements • A zodiac calendar **Writing Task** • Write about events at your school or in your city **WRITING BOOSTER** Guided writing practice
• Acknowledge a compliment with Thank you • Apologize with I'm sorry when expressing disappointing information • Use That's too bad to express disappointment • Use What about you? to ask for someone's opinion • Use Well to soften a strong opinion	**Listening Tasks** • Confirm details about clothes • Determine colors of garments **Pronunciation** • Plural nouns	**Reading Texts** • A sales flyer from a department store **Writing Task** • Write sentences about the clothes you have, need, want, and like **WRITING BOOSTER** Guided writing practice
• Say Me? to give yourself time to think of a personal response • Use Well to introduce a lengthy response • Use What about you? to ask for parallel information • Use So to introduce a conversation topic • Use How about you? to ask for parallel information • Say Sure to indicate a willingness to answer • Begin a response to an unexpected question with Oh	**Listening Task** • Match chores to the people who performed them **Pronunciation** • Third-person singular verb endings	**Reading Text** • A review of housekeeping robots **Writing Task** • Describe your typical week, using adverbs of frequency and time expressions **WRITING BOOSTER** Guided writing practice

v

	COMMUNICATION GOALS	VOCABULARY	GRAMMAR

UNIT 8
Home and Neighborhood
PAGE 64
	• Describe your neighborhood
	• Ask about someone's home
	• Talk about furniture and appliances
		• Buildings
		• Places in the neighborhood
		• Rooms
		• Furniture and appliances
		VOCABULARY BOOSTER
		• More home and office vocabulary
			• The simple present tense:
			  ◦ Questions with <u>Where</u>, prepositions of place
			• <u>There is</u> and <u>there are</u>:
			  ◦ Statements and <u>yes</u> / <u>no</u> questions
			  ◦ Contractions and common errors
			• Questions with <u>How many</u>
			GRAMMAR BOOSTER Extra practice

UNIT 9
Activities and Plans
PAGE 72
	• Describe today's weather
	• Discuss plans
	• Ask about people's activities
		• Weather expressions
		• Present and future time expressions
		VOCABULARY BOOSTER
		• More weather vocabulary / seasons
			• The present continuous:
			  ◦ Statements: form and usage
			  ◦ <u>Yes</u> / <u>no</u> questions
			  ◦ Information questions
			  ◦ For future plans
			• The present participle: spelling rules
			GRAMMAR BOOSTER Extra practice

UNIT 10 **Food** PAGE 80	• Discuss ingredients for a recipe • Offer and ask for foods • Invite someone to join you at the table	• Foods and drinks • Places to keep food in a kitchen • Containers and quantities • Cooking verbs **VOCABULARY BOOSTER** • More vegetables and fruits	• <u>How much</u> / <u>Are there any</u> • Count nouns and non-count nouns • <u>How much</u> / <u>Is there any</u> **GRAMMAR BOOSTER** Extra practice

UNIT 11
Past Events
PAGE 88
	• Tell someone about an event
	• Describe your past activities
	• Talk about your weekend
		• Past-time expressions
		• Outdoor activities
		VOCABULARY BOOSTER
		• More outdoor activities
			• The past tense of be; <u>There was</u> / <u>there were</u>:
			  ◦ Statements, questions, and contractions
			• The simple past tense
			  ◦ Regular verbs, irregular verbs
			  ◦ Statements, questions, and short answers
			GRAMMAR BOOSTER Extra practice

UNIT 12 **Appearance and Health** PAGE 96	• Describe appearance • Show concern about an injury • Suggest a remedy	• Adjectives to describe hair • The face • Parts of the body • Accidents and injuries • Ailments, remedies **VOCABULARY BOOSTER** • More parts of the body	• Describing people with <u>be</u> and <u>have</u> • <u>Should</u> + base form for suggestions **GRAMMAR BOOSTER** Extra practice
UNIT 13 **Abilities and Requests** PAGE 104	• Discuss your abilities • Politely decline an invitation • Ask for and agree to do a favor	• Abilities • Adverbs <u>well</u> and <u>badly</u> • Reasons for not doing something • Favors **VOCABULARY BOOSTER** • More musical instruments	• <u>Can</u> and <u>can't</u> for ability • <u>Too</u> + adjective, common errors • Polite requests with <u>Could you</u> + base form **GRAMMAR BOOSTER** Extra practice
UNIT 14 **Life Events and Plans** PAGE 112 **Units 8–14 Review** PAGE 120	• Get to know someone's life story • Discuss plans • Share your dreams for the future	• Some life events • Academic subjects • More leisure activities • Some dreams for the future **VOCABULARY BOOSTER** • More academic subjects • More leisure activities	• <u>Be going to</u> + base form **GRAMMAR BOOSTER** Extra practice

Countries and nationalities, Numbers 100 to 1,000,000,000, Irregular verbs, Pronunciation table .... page 124

Vocabulary Booster .... page 129
Grammar Booster .... page 140

CONVERSATION STRATEGIES	LISTENING / PRONUNCIATION	READING / WRITING
• Begin a question with <u>And</u> to indicate you want additional information • Use <u>Really?</u> to introduce contradictory information • Use <u>Well</u> to indicate you are deciding how to begin a response • Respond positively to a description with <u>Sounds nice!</u> • Use <u>Actually</u> to introduce an opinion that might surprise • Say <u>I don't know. I'm not sure</u> to avoid making a direct negative statement	**Listening Tasks** • Determine the best house or apartment for clients of a real estate company • Complete statements about locations of furniture and appliances **Pronunciation** • Linking sounds	**Reading Texts** • House and apartment rental listings • Descriptions of people and their homes **Writing Task** • Compare and contrast your home with other homes **WRITING BOOSTER** Guided writing practice
• Use <u>Hi</u> and <u>Hey</u> to greet people informally • Say <u>No kidding!</u> to show surprise • Use <u>So</u> to introduce a conversation topic • Answer the phone with <u>Hello?</u> • Identify yourself with <u>This is</u> on the phone • Use <u>Well, actually</u> to begin an excuse • Say <u>Oh, I'm sorry</u> after interrupting • Say <u>Talk to you later</u> to indicate the end of a phone conversation	**Listening Tasks** • Determine weather and temperatures in cities in a weather report • Complete statements about people's activities, using the present continuous **Pronunciation** • Rising and falling intonation of <u>yes</u> / <u>no</u> and information questions	**Reading Texts** • A daily planner • The weather forecast for four cities **Writing Task** • Write about plans for the week, using the present continuous **WRITING BOOSTER** Guided writing practice
• Say <u>I'll check</u> to indicate you'll get information for someone • Decline an offer politely with <u>No, thanks</u> • Use <u>Please pass the</u> to ask for something at the table • Say <u>Here you go</u> as you offer something • Say <u>Nice to see you</u> to greet someone you already know • Use <u>You too</u> to repeat a greeting politely	**Listening Task** • Identify the foods discussed in conversations **Pronunciation** • Vowel sounds: /i/, /ɪ/, /eɪ/, /ɛ/, /æ/	**Reading Texts** • Recipe cards • A weekly schedule **Writing Task** • Write about what you eat in a typical day **WRITING BOOSTER** Guided writing practice
• Ask <u>Why?</u> to ask for a clearer explanation • Use <u>What about?</u> to ask for more information • Use a double question to clarify • Use <u>just</u> to minimize the importance of an action • Say <u>Let me think</u> to gain time to answer • Say <u>Oh yeah</u> to indicate you just remembered something	**Listening Tasks** • Circle the year you hear • Infer the correct day or month • Choose activities mentioned in conversations **Pronunciation** • Simple past tense regular verb endings	**Reading Text** • A blog in which people describe what they did the previous weekend **Writing Task** • Write about the activities of two people, based on a complex picture • Write about your weekend and what you did **WRITING BOOSTER** Guided writing practice
• Use <u>Oh</u> to indicate you've understood • Say <u>No kidding</u> to show surprise • Say <u>I'm sorry to hear that</u>, <u>Oh, no</u>, and <u>That's too bad</u> to express sympathy • Use <u>Actually</u> to introduce an opinion that might surprise • Use <u>What's wrong?</u> to ask about an illness • Use <u>really</u> to intensify advice with should • Respond to good advice with <u>Good idea</u> • Say <u>I hope you feel better</u> when someone feels sick	**Listening Tasks** • Identify the people described in conversations • Complete statements about injuries • Identify the ailments and remedies suggested in conversations **Pronunciation** • More vowel sounds	**Reading Text** • A magazine article about two celebrities **Writing Task** • Write a description of someone you know **WRITING BOOSTER** Guided writing practice
• Use <u>Actually</u> to give information • Use <u>Really?</u> to show surprise or interest • Suggest a shared course of action with <u>Let's</u> • Politely decline a suggestion with <u>I'm really sorry but</u> and a reason • Accept a refusal with <u>Maybe some other time</u> • Use <u>Sure</u> and <u>No problem</u> to agree to someone's request for a favor	**Listening Task** • Complete requests for favors **Pronunciation** • Blending of sounds: <u>Could you</u>	**Reading Text** • An article about infant-toddler development **Writing Task** • Describe things people can and can't do when they get old **WRITING BOOSTER** Guided writing practice
• Use <u>And you?</u> to show interest in another person • Use <u>Not really</u> to soften a negative response • Ask <u>What about you?</u> to extend the conversation • Use <u>Well</u> and <u>Actually</u> to explain or clarify	**Listening Tasks** • Choose correct statements • Circle correct words or phrases • Complete statements about activities, using the present continuous • Infer people's wishes for the future **Pronunciation** • Diphthongs	**Reading Text** • A short biography of Harry Houdini **Writing Task** • Write your own illustrated life story, including plans and dreams for the future **WRITING BOOSTER** Guided writing practice

Writing Booster .... page 148   Top Notch Pop Lyrics .... page 150

TO THE TEACHER

What is *Top Notch*?

Top Notch is a six-level* communicative course that prepares adults and young adults to interact successfully and confidently with both native and non-native speakers of English.

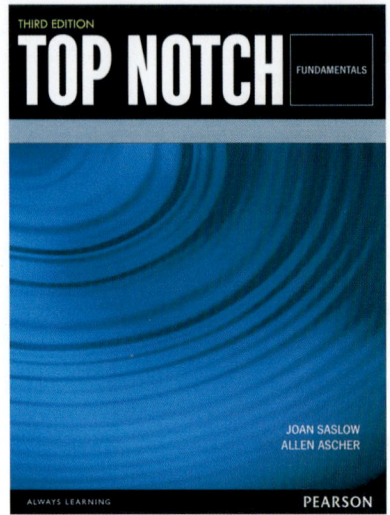

The goal of *Top Notch* is to make English unforgettable through:
- Multiple exposures to new language
- Numerous opportunities to practice it
- Deliberate and intensive recycling

The *Top Notch* course has two beginning levels—*Top Notch Fundamentals* for true beginners and *Top Notch 1* for false beginners. *Top Notch* is benchmarked to the Global Scale of English and is tightly correlated to the Can-do Statements of the Common European Framework of Reference.

Each full level of *Top Notch* contains material for 60–90 hours of classroom instruction. In addition, the entire course can be tailored to blended learning with an integrated online component, *MyEnglishLab*.

NEW This third edition of *Top Notch* includes these new features: Extra Grammar Exercises, digital full-color Vocabulary Flash Cards, Conversation Activator videos, Pronunciation Coach videos, and a Writing Booster.

* Summit 1 and *Summit 2* are the titles of the 5th and 6th levels of the *Top Notch* course.

Award-Winning Instructional Design*

Daily confirmation of progress

Each easy-to-follow two-page lesson begins with a clearly stated practical communication goal closely allied to the Common European Framework's Can-do Statements. All activities are integrated with the goal, giving vocabulary and grammar meaning and purpose. *Now You Can* activities ensure that students achieve each goal and confirm their progress in every class session.

True-beginner vocabulary and grammar

Clear captioned picture-dictionary illustrations with accompanying audio take the guesswork out of meaning and pronunciation. Grammar presentations clarify form, meaning, and use. The unique *Recycle this Language* feature continually puts known words and grammar in front of students' eyes as they communicate, to make sure language remains active. A new Writing Booster in the back of the Student's Book provides guided writing practice that incorporates vocabulary and grammar from the unit.

Authentic social language

Even beginning students should learn appealing natural social language. Forty-two memorable Conversation Models provide lively controlled conversation practice that ensures enthusiasm and motivation.

Active listening syllabus

All Vocabulary presentations, Pronunciation presentations, Conversation Models, Listening Comprehension exercises, and Readings are recorded on the audio, ensuring that students develop good pronunciation, intonation, and auditory memory. In addition, approximately fifty tasks specifically developed for beginning learners develop fundamental comprehension skills.

We wish you and your students enjoyment and success with *Top Notch Fundamentals*. We wrote it for you.

Joan Saslow and Allen Ascher

* Top Notch is the recipient of the Association of Educational Publishers' *Distinguished Achievement Award*.

COMPONENTS

ActiveTeach

Maximize the impact of your *Top Notch* lessons. This digital tool provides an interactive classroom experience that can be used with or without an interactive whiteboard (IWB). It includes a full array of digital and printable features.

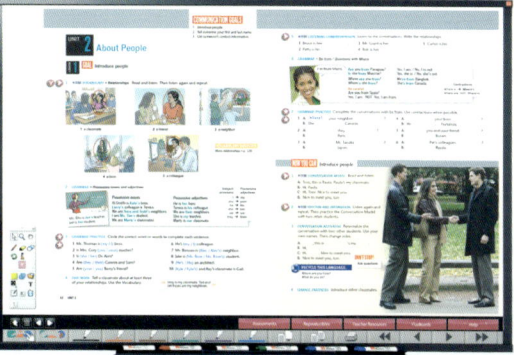

For class presentation...

- 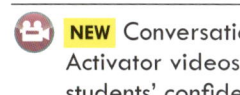 **NEW** Conversation Activator videos: increase students' confidence in oral communication
- 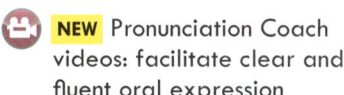 **NEW** Pronunciation Coach videos: facilitate clear and fluent oral expression
- 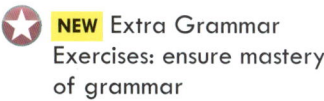 **NEW** Extra Grammar Exercises: ensure mastery of grammar
- **NEW** Digital Full-Color Vocabulary Flash Cards: accelerate retention of new vocabulary

PLUS

- Clickable Audio: instant access to the complete classroom audio program
- *Top Notch TV* Video Program: a hilarious sitcom and authentic on-the-street interviews
- *Top Notch Pop* Songs and Karaoke: original songs for additional language practice

For planning...

- A *Methods Handbook* for a communicative classroom
- Detailed timed lesson plans for each two-page lesson
- *Top Notch TV* teaching notes
- Complete answer keys, audio scripts, and video scripts

For extra support...

- Hundreds of extra printable activities, with teaching notes
- *Top Notch Pop* language exercises
- *Top Notch TV* activity worksheets

For assessment...

- Ready-made unit and review Achievement Tests with options to edit, add, or delete items.

MyEnglishLab
An optional online learning tool

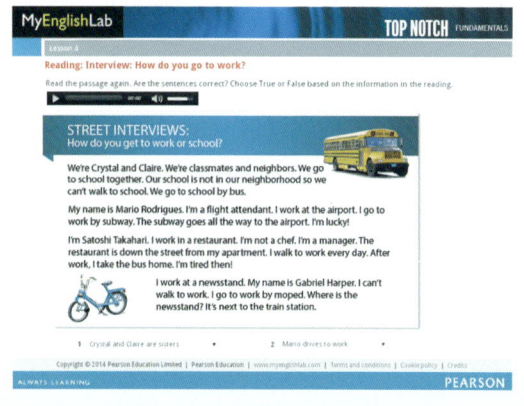

- **NEW** Grammar Coach videos plus the Pronunciation Coach videos, and Digital Vocabulary Flash Cards
- **NEW** Immediate meaningful feedback on wrong answers
- **NEW** Remedial grammar exercises
- Interactive practice of all material presented in the course
- Grade reports that display performance and time on task
- Auto-graded Achievement Tests

Workbook
Lesson-by-lesson written exercises to accompany the Student's Book

Full-Course Placement Tests
Choose printable or online version

Classroom Audio Program

- A set of Audio CDs, as an alternative to the clickable audio in the ActiveTeach
- Contains a variety of authentic regional and non-native accents to build comprehension of diverse English speakers
- **NEW** A downloadable Audio App for students allows access anytime, anywhere

Teacher's Edition and Lesson Planner

- Detailed interleaved lesson plans, language and culture notes, answer keys, and more
- Includes ActiveTeach on DVD-ROM, with hundreds of extra printable activities

For more information: www.pearsonelt.com/topnotch3e

ABOUT THE AUTHORS

Joan Saslow

Joan Saslow has taught in a variety of programs in South America and the United States. She is author or coauthor of a number of widely used courses, some of which are *Ready to Go, Workplace Plus, Literacy Plus,* and *Summit*. She is also author of *English in Context,* a series for reading science and technology. Ms. Saslow was the series director of *True Colors* and *True Voices*. She has participated in the English Language Specialist Program in the U.S. Department of State's Bureau of Educational and Cultural Affairs.

Allen Ascher

Allen Ascher has been a teacher and teacher trainer in China and the United States, as well as academic director of the intensive English program at Hunter College. Mr. Ascher has also been an ELT publisher and was responsible for publication and expansion of numerous well-known courses including *True Colors, NorthStar,* the *Longman TOEFL Preparation Series,* and the *Longman Academic Writing Series*. He is coauthor of *Summit* and he wrote the "Teaching Speaking" module of *Teacher Development Interactive,* an online multimedia teacher-training program.

Ms. Saslow and Mr. Ascher are frequent presenters at professional conferences and have been coauthoring courses for teens, adults, and young adults since 2002.

AUTHORS' ACKNOWLEDGMENTS

The authors are indebted to these reviewers, who provided extensive and detailed feedback and suggestions for *Top Notch,* as well as the hundreds of teachers who completed surveys and participated in groups.

Manuel Wilson Alvarado Miles, Quito, Ecuador • **Shirley Ando,** Otemae University, Hyogo, Japan • **Vanessa de Andrade,** CCBEU Inter Americano, Curitiba, Brazil • **Miguel Arrazola,** CBA, Santa Cruz, Bolivia • **Mark Barta,** Proficiency School of English, São Paulo, Brazil • **Edwin Bello,** PROULEX, Guadalajara, Mexico • **Mary Blum,** CBA, Cochabamba, Bolivia • **María Elizabeth Boccia,** Proficiency School of English, São Paulo, Brazil • **Pamela Cristina Borja Baltán,** Quito, Ecuador • **Eliana Anabel L. Buccia,** AMICANA, Mendoza, Argentina • **José Humberto Calderón Díaz,** CALUSAC, Guatemala City, Guatemala • **María Teresa Calienes Csirke,** Idiomas Católica, Lima, Peru • **Esther María Carbo Morales,** Quito, Ecuador • **Jorge Washington Cárdenas Castillo,** Quito, Ecuador • **Eréndira Yadira Carrera García,** UVM Chapultepec, Mexico City, Mexico • **Viviane de Cássia Santos Carlini,** Spectrum Line, Pouso Alegre, Brazil • **Centro Colombo Americano,** Bogota, Colombia • **Guven Ciftci,** Fatih University, Istanbul, Turkey • **Diego Cisneros,** CBA, Tarija, Bolivia • **Paul Crook,** Meisei University, Tokyo, Japan • **Alejandra Díaz Loo,** El Cultural, Arequipa, Peru • **Jesús G. Díaz Osío,** Florida National College, Miami, USA • **María Eid Ceneviva,** CBA, Bolivia • **Amalia Elvira Rodríguez Espinoza De Los Monteros,** Guayaquil, Ecuador • **María Argelia Estrada Vásquez,** CALUSAC, Guatemala City, Guatemala • **John Fieldeldy,** College of Engineering, Nihon University, Aizuwakamatsu-shi, Japan • **Marleni Humbelina Flores Urízar,** CALUSAC, Guatemala City, Guatemala • **Gonzalo Fortune,** CBA, Sucre, Bolivia • **Andrea Fredricks,** Embassy CES, San Francisco, USA • **Irma Gallegos Peláez,** UVM Tlalpan, Mexico City, Mexico • **Alberto Gamarra,** CBA, Santa Cruz, Bolivia • **María Amparo García Peña,** ICPNA Cusco, Peru • **Amanda Gillis-Furutaka,** Kyoto Sangyo University, Kyoto, Japan • **Martha Angelina González Párraga,** Guayaquil, Ecuador • **Octavio Garduño Ruiz,** Business Training Consultant, Mexico City, Mexico • **Ralph Grayson,** Idiomas Católica, Lima, Peru • **Murat Gultekin,** Fatih University, Istanbul, Turkey • **Oswaldo Gutiérrez,** PROULEX, Guadalajara, Mexico • **Ayaka Hashinishi,** Otemae University, Hyogo, Japan • **Alma Lorena Hernández de Armas,** CALUSAC, Guatemala City, Guatemala • **Kent Hill,** Seigakuin University, Saitama-ken, Japan • **Kayoko Hirao,** Nichii Gakkan Company, COCO Juku, Japan • **Jesse Huang,** National Central University, Taoyuan, Taiwan • **Eric Charles Jones,** Seoul University of Technology, Seoul, South Korea • **Jun-Chen Kuo,** Tajen University, Pingtung, Taiwan • **Susan Krieger,** Embassy CES, San Francisco, USA • **Ana María de la Torre Ugarte,** ICPNA Chiclayo, Peru • **Erin Lemaistre,** Chung-Ang University, Seoul, South Korea • **Eleanor S. Leu,** Soochow University, Taipei, Taiwan • **Yihui Li (Stella Li),** Fooyin University, Kaohsiung, Taiwan • **Chin-Fan Lin,** Shih Hsin University, Taipei, Taiwan • **Linda Lin,** Tatung Institute of Technology, Taiwan • **Kristen Lindblom,** Embassy CES, San Francisco, USA • **Patricio David López Logacho,** Quito, Ecuador • **Diego López Tasara,** Idiomas Católica, Lima, Peru • **Neil Macleod,** Kansai Gaidai University, Osaka, Japan • **Adriana Marcés,** Idiomas Católica, Lima, Peru • **Robyn McMurray,** Pusan National University, Busan, South Korea • **Paula Medina,** London Language Institute, London, Canada • **Juan Carlos Muñoz,** American School Way, Bogota, Colombia • **Noriko Mori,** Otemae University, Hyogo, Japan • **Adrián Esteban Narváez Pacheco,** Cuenca, Ecuador • **Tim Newfields,** Tokyo University Faculty of Economics, Tokyo, Japan • **Ana Cristina Ochoa,** CCBEU Inter Americano, Curitiba, Brazil • **Tania Elizabeth Ortega Santacruz,** Cuenca, Ecuador • **Martha Patricia Páez,** Quito, Ecuador • **María de Lourdes Pérez Valdespino,** Universidad del Valle de México, Mexico • **Wahrena Elizabeth Pfeister,** University of Suwon, Gyeonggi-Do, South Korea • **Wayne Allen Pfeister,** University of Suwon, Gyeonggi-Do, South Korea • **Andrea Rebonato,** CCBEU Inter Americano, Curitiba, Brazil • **Thomas Robb,** Kyoto Sangyo University, Kyoto, Japan • **Mehran Sabet,** Seigakuin University, Saitama-ken, Japan • **Majid Safadaran Mosazadeh,** ICPNA Chiclayo, Peru • **Timothy Samuelson,** BridgeEnglish, Denver, USA • **Héctor Sánchez,** PROULEX, Guadalajara, Mexico • **Mónica Alexandra Sánchez Escalante,** Quito, Ecuador • **Jorge Mauricio Sánchez Montalván,** Quito, Universidad Politécnica Salesiana (UPS), Ecuador • **Letícia Santos,** ICBEU Ibiá, Brazil • **Elena Sapp,** INTO Oregon State University, Corvallis, USA • **Robert Sheridan,** Otemae University, Hyogo, Japan • **John Eric Sherman,** Hong Ik University, Seoul, South Korea • **Brooks Slaybaugh,** Asia University, Tokyo, Japan • **João Vitor Soares,** NACC, São Paulo, Brazil • **Silvia Solares,** CBA, Sucre, Bolivia • **Chayawan Sonchaeng,** Delaware County Community College, Media, PA • **María Julia Suárez,** CBA, Cochabamba, Bolivia • **Elena Sudakova,** English Language Center, Kiev, Ukraine • **Richard Swingle,** Kansai Gaidai College, Osaka, Japan • **Blanca Luz Terrazas Zamora,** ICPNA Cusco, Peru • **Sandrine Ting,** St. John's University, New Taipei City, Taiwan • **Christian Juan Torres Medina,** Guayaquil, Ecuador • **Raquel Torrico,** CBA, Sucre, Bolivia • **Jessica Ueno,** Otemae University, Hyogo, Japan • **Ximena Vacaflor C.,** CBA, Tarija, Bolivia • **René Valdivia Pereira,** CBA, Santa Cruz, Bolivia • **Solange Lopes Vinagre Costa,** SENAC, São Paulo, Brazil • **Magno Alejandro Vivar Hurtado,** Cuenca, Ecuador • **Dr. Wen-hsien Yang,** National Kaohsiung Hospitality College, Kaohsiung, Taiwan • **Juan Zárate,** El Cultural, Arequipa, Peru

COMMUNICATION GOALS

1 Describe your neighborhood.
2 Ask about someone's home.
3 Talk about furniture and appliances.

UNIT 8 Home and Neighborhood

LESSON 1 GOAL Describe your neighborhood

DIGITAL FLASH CARDS

1 ▶3:19 **VOCABULARY** • ***Buildings*** Read and listen. Then listen again and repeat.

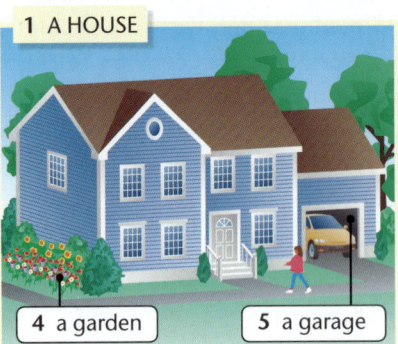

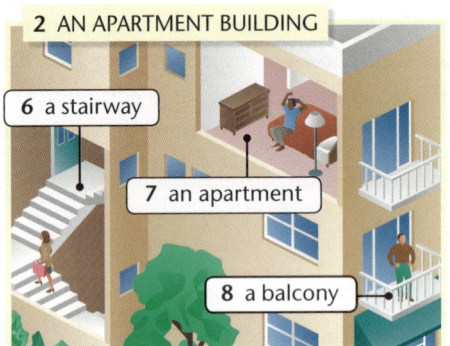

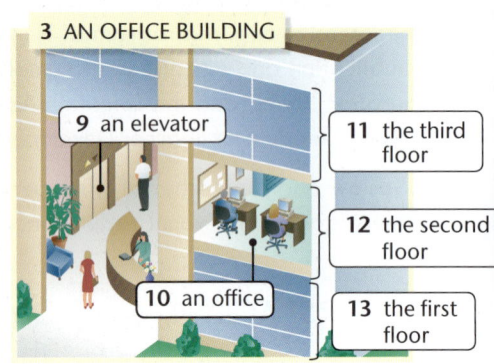

1 A HOUSE
4 a garden
5 a garage
2 AN APARTMENT BUILDING
6 a stairway
7 an apartment
8 a balcony
3 AN OFFICE BUILDING
9 an elevator
10 an office
11 the third floor
12 the second floor
13 the first floor

2 **GRAMMAR** • ***The simple present tense: questions with <u>Where</u> / Prepositions of place***

Questions with <u>Where</u>

Where **do** you **live**?
Where **do** your parents **live**?

Where **does** he **work**?
Where **does** your mother **work**?

Prepositions of place

in	at	on
She lives **in** an apartment.	I live **at** 50 Main Street.	Her house is **on** Bank Street.
They live **in** a house.	He works **at** a bookstore.	We go to school **on** 34th Avenue.
I work **in** an office.	They study **at** the Brooke School.	I work **on** the tenth floor.

3 **GRAMMAR PRACTICE** Complete the conversations. Use the simple present tense and prepositions of place.

1 A: Where .... your sister ....?
B: She lives .... an apartment.

2 A: Where .... you .... English?
B: We study .... the school around the corner.

3 A: Where .... your neighbor ....?
B: She works .... a bookstore.

4 A: Where .... your parents ....?
B: They live .... 58 Gray Street.

DIGITAL MORE EXERCISES

DIGITAL VIDEO COACH

4 ▶3:20 **PRONUNCIATION** • ***Linking sounds*** Read and listen. Then listen and repeat.

1 It's on the second floor.
2 She works in an office.
3 He lives in an apartment.
4 My apartment has a balcony.

5 **VOCABULARY / GRAMMAR PRACTICE** With a partner, ask and answer questions with Where. Use the simple present tense.

" Where do you live? "

6 ▶ 3:21 **VOCABULARY • *Places in the neighborhood*** Read and listen. Then listen again and repeat.

" I live on Main Street. "

▶ 3:22 Preposition **near**

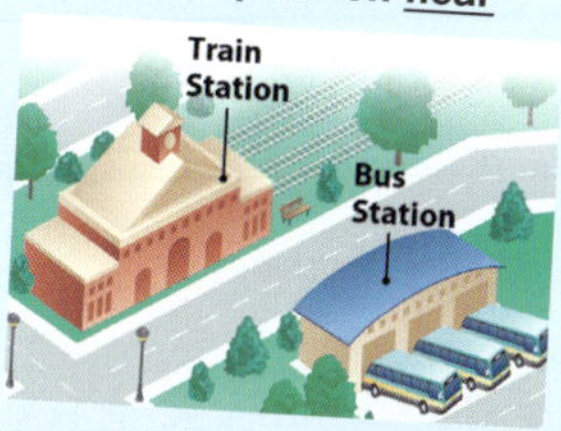

The train station is **near** the bus station. It's right across the street.

1 a bus station   2 a train station   3 a stadium

    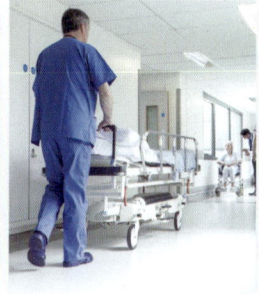

4 a park   5 a mall   6 a museum   7 an airport   8 a hospital

NOW YOU CAN   Describe your neighborhood

1 ▶ 3:23 **CONVERSATION MODEL** Read and listen.

A: Do you live far from here?
B: No. About fifteen minutes by bus.
A: And is the neighborhood nice?
B: Yes, it is. My apartment is near a park and a mall.
A: Really? My apartment is next to an airport.

2 ▶ 3:24 **RHYTHM AND INTONATION** Listen again and repeat. Then practice the Conversation Model with a partner.

3 **CONVERSATION ACTIVATOR** With a partner, personalize the conversation.

A: Do you live far from here?
B: ....
A: And is the neighborhood nice?
B: ...., it .... My .... is ....
A: Really? My .... is ....

DON'T STOP!
Ask more questions.
Are there [good restaurants / museums]?
Where do you [go shopping / go out for dinner]?
And where do you [work]?

4 **CHANGE PARTNERS** Ask about another classmate's neighborhood.

LESSON 2 — GOAL: Ask about someone's home

1 ▶ 3:25 **VOCABULARY** • *Rooms* Read and listen. Then listen again and repeat.

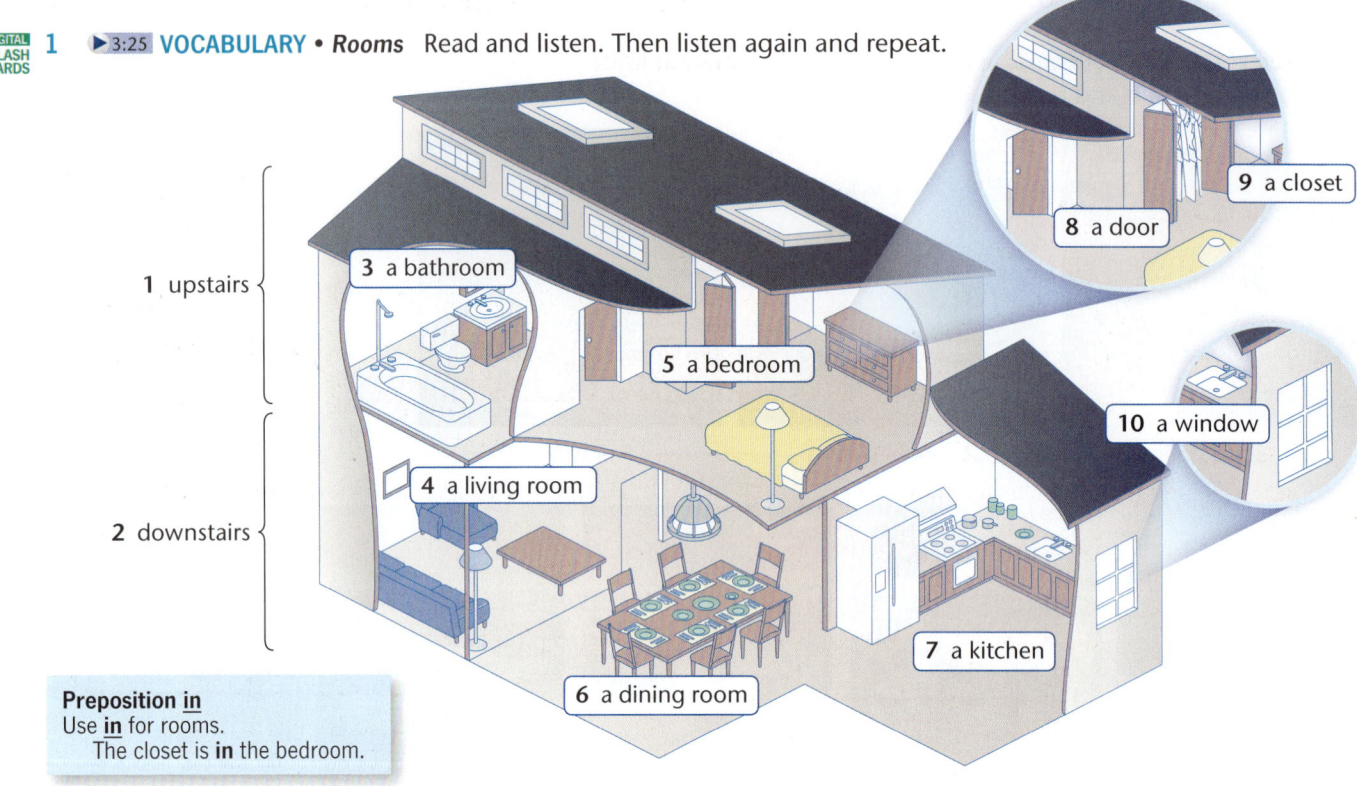

Preposition in
Use **in** for rooms.
The closet is **in** the bedroom.

2 PAIR WORK Tell your partner about the rooms in your home.

" My apartment has one large bedroom and two small bedrooms. "

3 GRAMMAR • *There is* and *There are* / Questions with *How many*

There is and **There are**
Use **There is** with singular nouns. Use **There are** with plural nouns.

There's a small bedroom downstairs.
There's a large closet and two windows.
There's no kitchen.

There are three large bedrooms upstairs.
There are two windows and a large closet.
There are no elevators.

Is there a balcony? | Yes, **there is**.
No, **there isn't**.

Are there closets? | Yes, **there are**.
No, **there aren't**.

Be careful!
There is → There's
BUT Yes, there is. NOT Yes, ~~there's~~.
There are NOT ~~There're~~

How many
Ask questions about quantity with **How many**. Always use a plural noun with **How many**.

How many bathrooms **are there**? (There are two.)
How many bedrooms **do** you **have**? (We have three.)

---

4 GRAMMAR PRACTICE Complete the sentences. Use <u>there's</u>, <u>there are</u>, <u>is there</u>, or <u>are there</u>.

1 How many closets *are there* in the house?
2 .... a small bedroom downstairs.
3 .... a balcony on the second floor?
4 .... an elevator and two stairways.
5 .... a garden next to her house.
6 .... two bedrooms upstairs.
7 .... a park near my apartment.
8 How many windows .... ?

5 **GRAMMAR PRACTICE** Write ten sentences about your house or apartment. Use There is and There are.

> *There's a small bathroom next to my bedroom.*

Ideas
- number of rooms
- size of rooms
- location of rooms

6 ▶ 3:26 **LISTENING COMPREHENSION** Listen to the conversations. Check the best house or apartment for each person.

Home Away from Home
Live in a house or apartment overseas for 1 to 6 months!
Call Us at 1-800-555-9038

1. **Paris**
☐ A two-bedroom house with a large kitchen
☐ A one-bedroom apartment with a small kitchen

2. **Buenos Aires**
☐ A two-bedroom house with three bathrooms
☐ A two-bedroom house with two bathrooms

3. **Tokyo**
☐ A one-bedroom apartment with a large kitchen
☐ A one-bedroom apartment with a large closet

4. **Montreal**
☐ A two-bedroom house with a small garden
☐ A two-bedroom apartment with a balcony

NOW YOU CAN Ask about someone's home

1 ▶ 3:27 **CONVERSATION MODEL** Read and listen.

A: Do you live in a house or an apartment?
B: An apartment.
A: What's it like?
B: Well, there are three large bedrooms, and it has a large kitchen.
A: Sounds nice!

2 ▶ 3:28 **RHYTHM AND INTONATION** Listen again and repeat. Then practice the Conversation Model with a partner.

3 **CONVERSATION ACTIVATOR** With a partner, personalize the conversation. Describe your house or apartment. Then change roles.

A: Do you live in a house or an apartment?
B: ……… .
A: What's it like?
B: Well, ……… .
A: Sounds nice!

DON'T STOP!
Ask more questions.
Is there ___ ? / Are there ___ ?
How many ___ are there?
Does your [house] have [a garage]?

4 **CHANGE PARTNERS** Talk about another classmate's home.

UNIT 8   67

LESSON 3 GOAL Talk about furniture and appliances

1 ▶3:29 **VOCABULARY** • *Furniture and appliances* First write the name of each room (a–f). Then read and listen. Listen again and repeat.

a an office

1 a printer
2 a computer
3 a desk

b

4 a dresser
5 a bed
6 a rug
7 a lamp

c

8 a toilet
9 a mirror
10 a shower
11 a sink
12 a bathtub

d

13 a table
14 a chair

e

15 a sofa
16 a bookcase
17 a TV

f
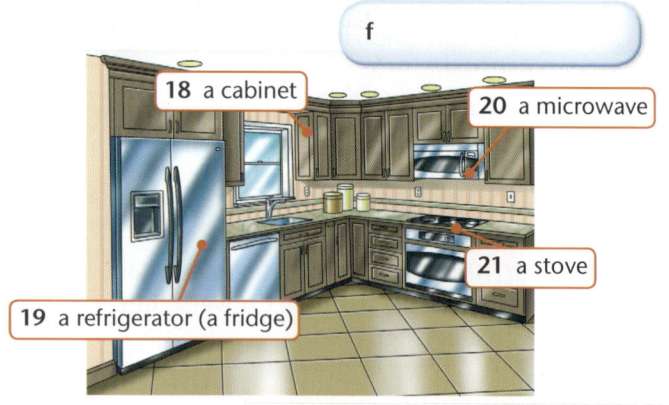
18 a cabinet
19 a refrigerator (a fridge)
20 a microwave
21 a stove

VOCABULARY BOOSTER
More home and office vocabulary • p. 129

2 ▶3:30 **LISTENING COMPREHENSION** Listen to the comments about furniture and appliances. Look at the pictures in the Vocabulary. Write the correct room.

1 It's in the ....
2 It's in the ....
3 It's in the ....
4 It's in the ....
5 They're in the ....
6 It's in the ....

3 **PAIR WORK** Ask your partner about the furniture and appliances in his or her home.

> ❝ What's in your living room? ❞

> ❝ My living room has a sofa and two chairs, and there's a large bookcase. ❞

NOW YOU CAN Talk about furniture and appliances

1 ▶ 3:31 **CONVERSATION MODEL** Read and listen.

   A: This is a nice sofa. What do you think?
   B: Actually, I think it's beautiful.
   A: And what about this lamp?
   B: I don't know. I'm not sure.

▶ 3:33
Positive and negative adjectives
☺ beautiful ☹ ugly
nice awful
great terrible

2 ▶ 3:32 **RHYTHM AND INTONATION** Listen again and repeat. Then practice the Conversation Model with a partner.

3 **CONVERSATION ACTIVATOR** Change the conversation. Ask your partner's opinion about the furniture and appliances in the pictures. (Or use your own pictures.) Then change roles.

   A: This is a nice ………. . What do you think?
   B: Actually, I think it's ………. .
   A: And what about this ………. ?
   B: ………. .

DON'T STOP!
Ask about other furniture and appliances.

RECYCLE THIS LANGUAGE.
I like this ___ .
I don't like this ___ .
Really?
What about you?

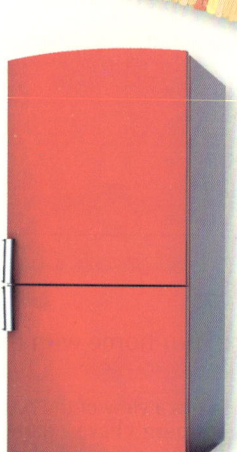

4 **CHANGE PARTNERS** Practice the conversation again.

UNIT 8   69

EXTENSION

1 ▶ 3:34 **READING** Read about where people live. Who lives in a house? Who lives in an apartment?

Where Do You Live?

Jeewhan Yoon

Tina Williams

Eduardo Calero

I'm Jeewhan Yoon from the city of Busan, in Korea. My wife and I live in a small house with two floors and a garage. There are two bedrooms, a living room, a small kitchen, and one bathroom.

My favorite room is the living room. There's a big sofa, and I usually read there. We also watch movies on TV in the living room.

One thing I don't like: we don't have a garden.

I'm Tina Williams, and I'm from Seattle, in the United States. I live in a small white house with a two-car garage.

Downstairs, there's a living room, a dining room, and a nice large kitchen with large windows and a view of the garden. There are two bedrooms and one bathroom upstairs. There's also a very small office—my favorite room. I study there.

It's small, but I love my house!

My name is Eduardo Calero, and I live in Caracas, Venezuela. My family has a really nice apartment on the eighth floor. There's an elevator, of course, and there's a garage on the first floor.

We have three bedrooms and two bathrooms. My brother and I have our own rooms. The kitchen is small, but it has beautiful new appliances. The living room is my favorite room, though, because it has a fantastic view of the city of Caracas.

2 **READING COMPREHENSION** Check the descriptions that match each person's home.

	Jeewhan Yoon	Tina Williams	Eduardo Calero
three bedrooms	☐	☐	☐
two bathrooms	☐	☐	☐
a small kitchen	☐	☐	☐
no office	☐	☐	☐
no garden	☐	☐	☐
a two-car garage	☐	☐	☐
an elevator	☐	☐	☐

DIGITAL
MORE EXERCISES

3 **PAIR WORK** Compare your home with the homes in the Reading.

> " Tina's kitchen has a view of the garden, but my house doesn't have a garden. "

> " Eduardo lives in an apartment. I live in an apartment, too. His apartment has two bathrooms, but my apartment has one. "

GRAMMAR BOOSTER
Unit 8 review • p. 140

For additional language practice...

♫ **TOP NOTCH POP** • Lyrics p. 150
"Home Is Where the Heart Is"

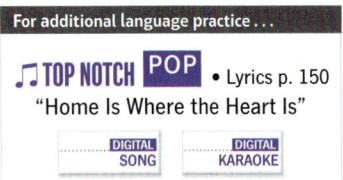

REVIEW

INFO GAP Find everything that's different in the two pictures. Ask questions. For example:
How many ___ are there?   Is there ___?
Does the ___ have ___?   Are there ___?

PAIR WORK

1 Express your opinions about the houses, the furniture, and the appliances. For example:
A: What do you think of ___?
B: I think it's really nice. What about you?

2 Your partner closes his or her book. You describe one of the houses. Your partner draws a picture of the house. For example:
Upstairs, there are two small bedrooms and a small bathroom.

WRITING Compare your home with one of the homes in the Reading on page 70. For example:

Ms. Williams's house has two
bedrooms upstairs, but my …

WRITING BOOSTER p. 148
Guidance for this writing exercise

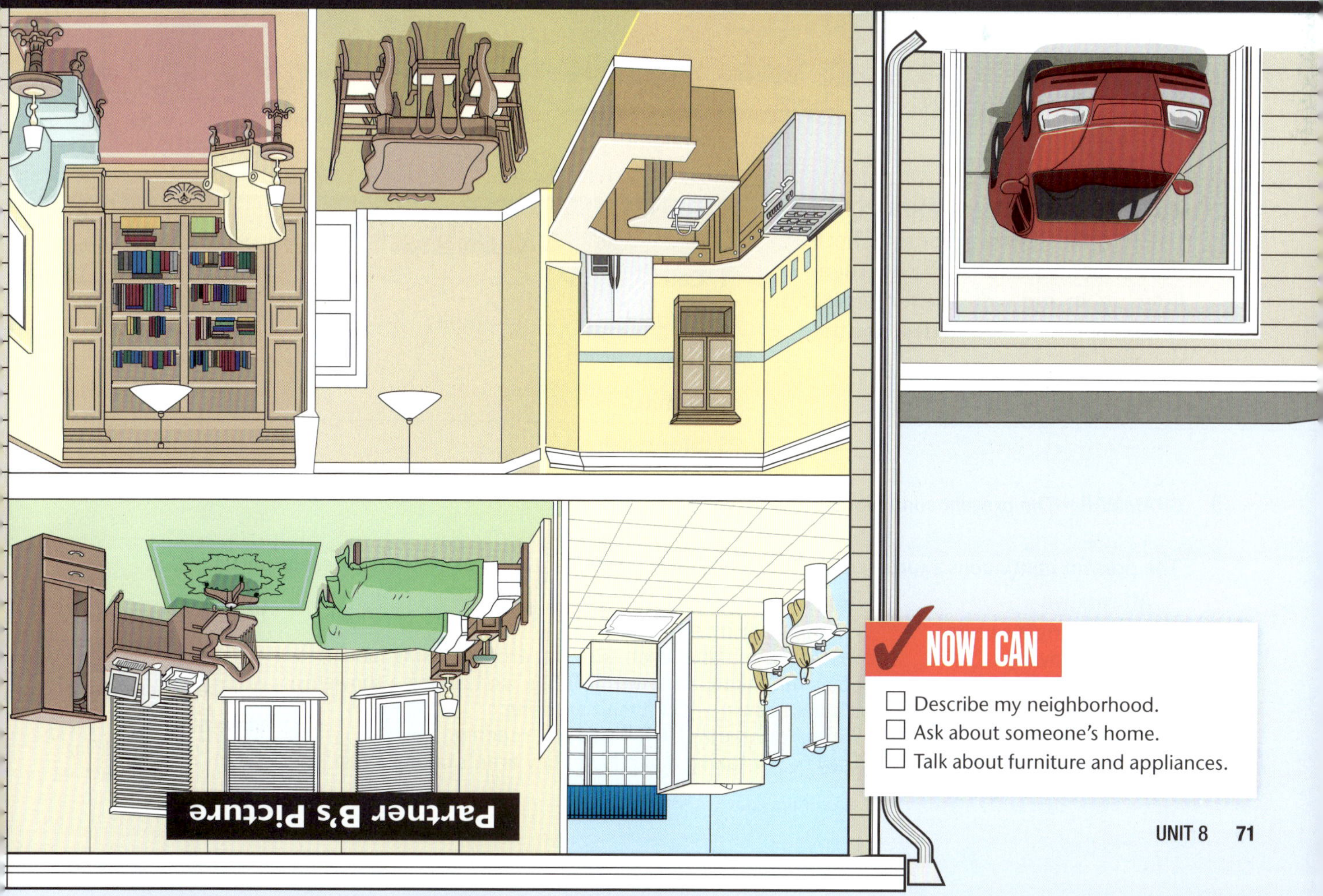

✓ **NOW I CAN**
☐ Describe my neighborhood.
☐ Ask about someone's home.
☐ Talk about furniture and appliances.

UNIT 8   71

UNIT 9 Activities and Plans

LESSON 1 **GOAL** Describe today's weather

VOCABULARY BOOSTER
More weather vocabulary • p. 130

COMMUNICATION GOALS
1 Describe today's weather.
2 Discuss plans.
3 Ask about people's activities.

1 ▶ 3:37 **VOCABULARY** • **Weather expressions** Read and listen. Then listen again and repeat.

HOW'S THE WEATHER?

1 It's sunny.

2 It's cloudy.

6 It's hot.

7 It's cold.

3 It's windy.

4 It's raining.

5 It's snowing.

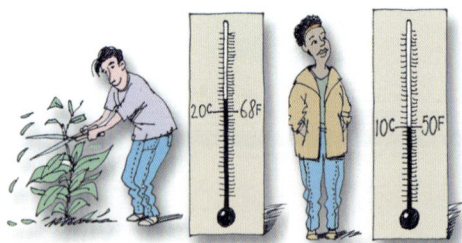

8 It's warm.   9 It's cool.

2 ▶ 3:38 **LISTENING COMPREHENSION**
Listen to the weather reports. Check the correct word for each city. Then listen again and write the temperatures. Finally, listen again and describe the weather.

City	Hot	Warm	Cool	Cold	What's the temperature?	How's the weather?
1 Cali	✓				35°	It's sunny.
2 Madrid						
3 Seoul						
4 Dubai						
5 Montreal						

3 **GRAMMAR** • *The present continuous: statements*

The present continuous expresses actions in progress now. Use a form of <u>be</u> and a present participle.

Affirmative
I'm wearing a sweater.
You're shaving.
She's taking a bath.
It's raining.
We're watching TV.
They're exercising.

Negative
I'm not wearing a jacket.
You're not making lunch. [OR You aren't making lunch.]
She's not taking a shower. [OR She isn't taking a shower.]
It's not snowing. [OR It isn't snowing.]
We're not reading. [OR We aren't reading.]
They're not taking a nap. [OR They aren't taking a nap.]

Present participles
wear → wearing
study → studying
exercise → exercising

Some others:
doing, listening, reading, working, meeting, getting

4 GRAMMAR • The present continuous: yes / no questions

Are you **eating** right now?	Yes, I am. / No, I'm not.
Is she **taking** the bus?	Yes, she is. / No, she's not. [OR No, she isn't.]
Is it **raining**?	Yes, it is. / No, it's not. [OR No, it isn't.]
Are they **walking**?	Yes, they are. / No, they're not. [OR No, they aren't.]

5 GRAMMAR PRACTICE   Complete each statement, question, or short answer with the present continuous. Use contractions.

1 .... now, and .... a nice, warm sweater.
   It / snow   *I / wear*

2 .... ? Yes, he .... his textbook.
   he /study   *He / read*

3 .... dinner right now. .... late at the office.
   Dad / not make   *He / work*

4 .... , and .... a shower.
   Jerome / exercise   *Ann / take*

5 .... TV. .... to music.
   The children / not watch   *They / listen*

6 .... this morning? No. It's cloudy and windy, but it ....
   it /rain   *not rain*

7 .... in the office right now? Yes, ...
   they / meet

a scarf

a coat

NOW YOU CAN   Describe today's weather

1 ▶3:39 **CONVERSATION MODEL** Read and listen.

   A: Hi, Molly. Jonathan.
   B: Hey, Jonathan. Where are you?
   A: I'm calling from Vancouver.
      How's the weather there in São Paulo?
   B: Today? Awful! It's raining and cold.
   A: No kidding! It's hot and sunny here.

   bad ☹
   Awful!
   Terrible!

   good ☺
   Nice!
   Great!
   Beautiful!

2 ▶3:40 **RHYTHM AND INTONATION** Listen again and repeat. Then practice the Conversation Model with a partner.

3 **CONVERSATION ACTIVATOR** With a partner, change the conversation. Choose two cities. Role-play a conversation about the weather there. (Option: Find the weather report in the newspaper, on TV, or online.) Then change roles.

   A: Hi, ...
   B: .... , ... Where are you?
   A: I'm calling from ....
      How's the weather there in .... ?
   B: Today? .... It's ....
   A: No kidding! It's .... here.

   DON'T STOP!
   Tell your partner what you're wearing.
      I'm wearing ___.
      I'm not wearing ___.

4 **CHANGE PARTNERS** Describe the weather in other places.

Lesson 2 GOAL Discuss plans

1 ▶ 3:41 **VOCABULARY** • *Present and future time expressions* Read and listen. Then listen again and repeat.

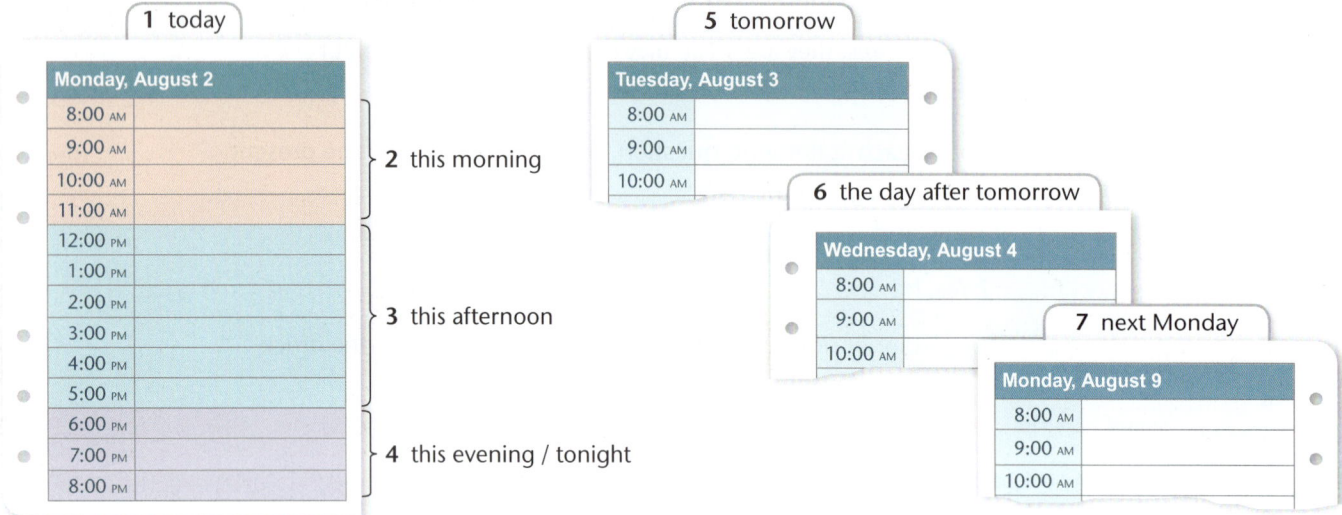

2 **GRAMMAR** • *The present continuous with present and future time expressions*

Actions in the present	Future plans
Are you watching TV **right now**?	I'm buying shoes **tomorrow**.
I'm not studying English **this year**.	They're cleaning the house **this weekend**, not today.
She's working at home **this week**.	Janet's meeting Bill **at 5:00 this afternoon**.

3 **GRAMMAR PRACTICE** Read Marissa Miller's date book for this week. Then complete the paragraph. Use the present continuous.

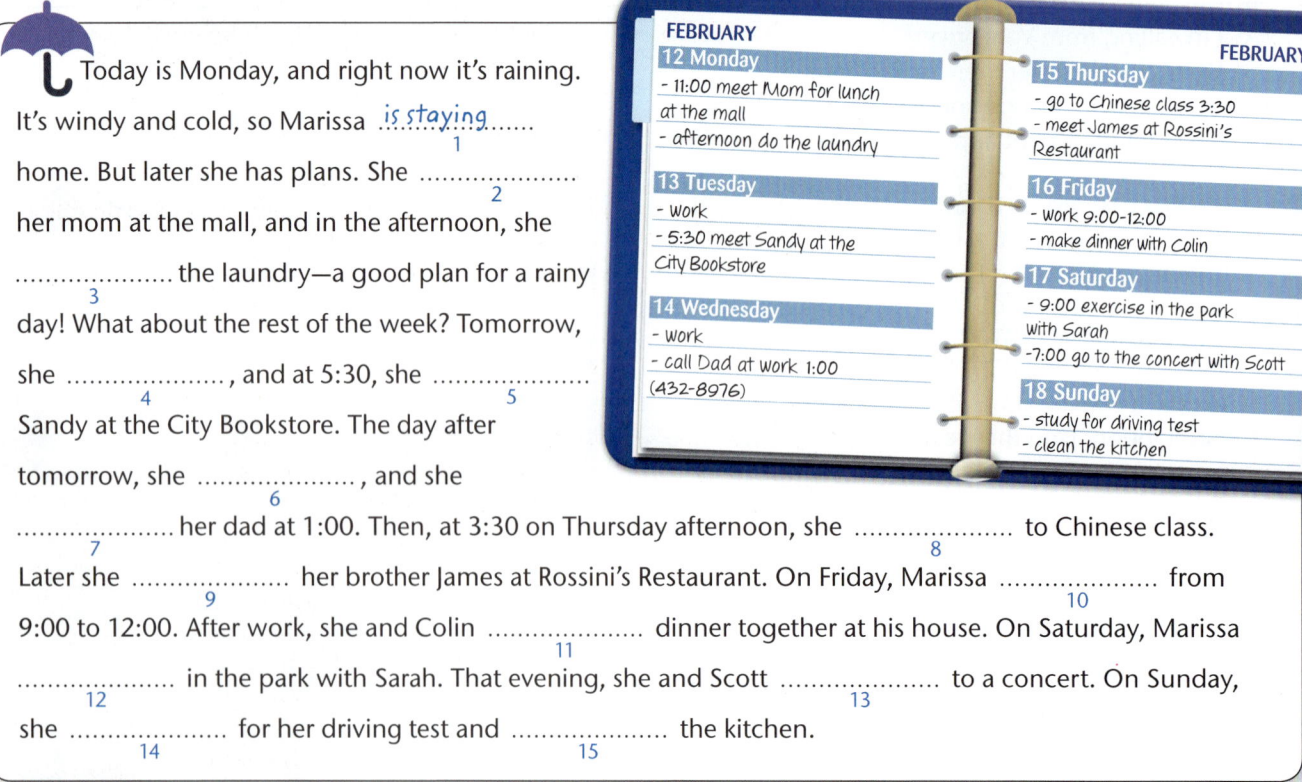

Today is Monday, and right now it's raining. It's windy and cold, so Marissa ..is staying.. (1) home. But later she has plans. She .... (2) her mom at the mall, and in the afternoon, she .... (3) the laundry—a good plan for a rainy day! What about the rest of the week? Tomorrow, she .... (4), and at 5:30, she .... (5) Sandy at the City Bookstore. The day after tomorrow, she .... (6), and she .... (7) her dad at 1:00. Then, at 3:30 on Thursday afternoon, she .... (8) to Chinese class. Later she .... (9) her brother James at Rossini's Restaurant. On Friday, Marissa .... (10) from 9:00 to 12:00. After work, she and Colin .... (11) dinner together at his house. On Saturday, Marissa .... (12) in the park with Sarah. That evening, she and Scott .... (13) to a concert. On Sunday, she .... (14) for her driving test and .... (15) the kitchen.

4 **PAIR WORK** Ask your partner yes / no questions about Marissa's schedule. Use the present continuous. Answer your partner's questions.

" Is Marissa exercising on Tuesday? "

NOW YOU CAN Discuss plans

1 ▶ 3:42 **CONVERSATION MODEL** Read and listen.

A: What beautiful weather! It's so sunny and warm!
B: It really is! . . . So, Kate, are you doing anything special this weekend?
A: Well, on Saturday, I'm meeting Pam in the park.
B: Do you want to get together on Sunday?
A: Sure! Call me Sunday morning, OK?

2 ▶ 3:43 **RHYTHM AND INTONATION** Listen again and repeat. Then practice the Conversation Model with a partner.

3 **PLAN YOUR CONVERSATION** Fill in the date book for this week. Write your activities and the times.

4 **CONVERSATION ACTIVATOR** With a partner, personalize the conversation with real information from your date books. Describe the weather today and use the time expressions for your plans. Then change roles.

A: What ……… weather! It's so ……… !
B: It really is! . . . So, ……… , are you doing anything special ……… ?
A: Well, ……… , I'm ……… .
B: Do you want to get together ……… ?
A: Sure! Call me ……… , OK?

DON'T STOP!
Ask about plans for other days of the week.

 RECYCLE THIS LANGUAGE.

Time expressions	Adjectives for weather		Describe the weather
on [Friday]	bad	good	It's so [cloudy / windy]!
this [afternoon]	awful	nice	And it's so [hot / cold / cool]!
in the [evening]	terrible	great	And it's [raining / snowing]!
tomorrow	ugly	beautiful	
the day after tomorrow			

5 **CHANGE PARTNERS** Discuss other plans.

UNIT 9   75

LESSON 3 | GOAL Ask about people's activities

1 GRAMMAR • The present continuous: information questions

What **is** she **watching**? (A TV program.)   What **are** you **doing**? (We're checking e-mail.)
Where **is** he **driving**? (To work.)   Where **are** they **going**? (They're going to the movies.)

BUT: Note the different word order when <u>who</u> is the subject.
Who **is working**? (Ben.)

2 PAIR WORK
Ask and answer questions about Mike and Patty. Use the present continuous and <u>What</u>, <u>Where</u>, and <u>Who</u>.

❝ It's 8:20. What's Mike doing? ❞

❝ He's eating breakfast. ❞

3 ▶ 3:44 PRONUNCIATION • Intonation of questions
Use rising intonation for <u>yes</u> / <u>no</u> questions. Use falling intonation for information questions. Read and listen. Then listen again and repeat.

Yes/no questions	Information questions
1 Are you eating? ↗	What are you eating? ↘
2 Is he walking? ↗	Where is he walking? ↘
3 Are they watching a movie? ↗	Who's watching a movie? ↘
4 Is her family at home? ↗	Where is her family? ↘
5 Are you a teacher? ↗	What do you do? ↘

4 GRAMMAR • The present participle: spelling rules

base form		present participle	base form		present participle
talk	→	talking	mak~~e~~	→	making
read	→	reading	tak~~e~~	→	taking
watch	→	watching	com~~e~~	→	coming

Remember:
shop → sho**pp**ing   get → ge**tt**ing   put → pu**tt**ing

76 UNIT 9

5 **GRAMMAR PRACTICE** Write the present participle of each base form.

1 check ....
2 write ....
3 wash ....
4 go ....
5 drive ....
6 get up ....

6 ▶ 3:45 **LISTENING COMPREHENSION** Listen. Complete each statement in the present continuous.

1 Sara's ....
2 Dan's ....
3 Eva's ....
4 Paul's ....
5 Marla's ....

NOW YOU CAN   Ask about people's activities

1 ▶ 3:46 **CONVERSATION MODEL** Read and listen.

A: Hello?
B: Hi, Grace. This is Jessica. What are you doing?
A: Well, actually, I'm doing the laundry right now.
B: Oh, I'm sorry. Should I call you back later?
A: Yes, thanks. Talk to you later. Bye.
B: Bye.

2 ▶ 3:47 **RHYTHM AND INTONATION** Listen again and repeat. Then practice the Conversation Model with a partner.

3 **CONVERSATION ACTIVATOR** With a partner, personalize the conversation. Use your own names. Use the pictures or use your own activities. Then change roles.

A: Hello?
B: Hi, ... This is .... What are you doing?
A: Well, actually, I .... right now.
B: Oh, I'm sorry. Should I call you back later?
A: Yes, thanks. Talk to you later. Bye.
B: ....

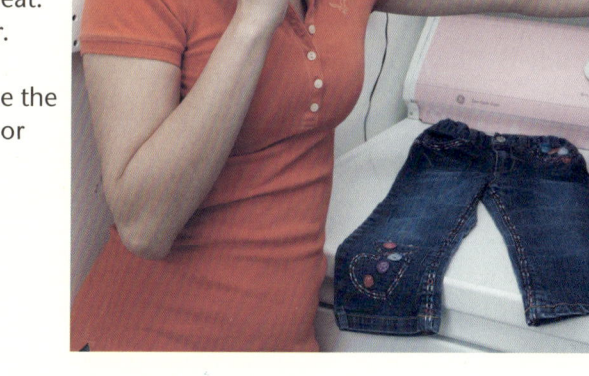

DON'T STOP!
Talk about a time to call back.
Call me at 3:00.
Call me tonight.

4 **CHANGE PARTNERS** Ask and talk about other activities.

EXTENSION

1 ▶ 3:48 **READING** Look at today's weather forecast.

2 **READING COMPREHENSION** Complete the chart for December 16th weather, according to the forecast in the Reading.

	in the morning	in the afternoon	in the evening
sunny	Guadalajara and Miami		
cloudy			
windy			
snowy			
rainy			
hot			
warm			
cold			
cool			

3 **READING COMPREHENSION** Look at the sunrise and sunset times. Answer the questions.

1 Which cities have sunrises before 7:30? ....
2 Which cities have sunsets before 5:00? ....

4 **VOCABULARY / GRAMMAR GAME** Team 1 mimes an activity. Team 2 asks questions. Use the activities from the box.

```
comb your hair      go to bed            check e-mail
drive               brush your teeth     listen to music
exercise            wash the dishes      put on makeup
talk on the phone   take out the garbage
get dressed
take a shower
read
watch TV
```

Are you putting on makeup?

GRAMMAR BOOSTER
Unit 9 review • p. 141

REVIEW

PAIR WORK Create telephone conversations for Sam and Debbie on Thursday and on Saturday. Ask about activities and plans. Ask about the weather. For example:

This afternoon I'm going shopping. Then tonight I'm ...

WRITING Write five sentences about your plans for this week. Use the present continuous. For example:

I'm going out for dinner on Saturday.

WRITING BOOSTER p. 148
Guidance for this writing exercise

Thursday, May 5, 1:20 P.M.

Saturday, May 7, 6:30 P.M.

✓ **NOW I CAN**
☐ Describe today's weather.
☐ Discuss plans.
☐ Ask about people's activities.

UNIT 10 Food

COMMUNICATION GOALS
1 Discuss ingredients for a recipe.
2 Offer and ask for foods.
3 Invite someone to join you at the table.

LESSON 1 GOAL Discuss ingredients for a recipe

1 ▶4:02 **VOCABULARY** • *Foods: count nouns* Read and listen. Then listen again and repeat.

1 an egg
2 an onion
3 an apple
4 an orange
5 a lemon
6 a banana
7 a tomato
8 a potato
9 a pepper
10 beans
11 peas

VOCABULARY BOOSTER
More vegetables and fruits • p. 131

2 ▶4:03 **LISTENING COMPREHENSION** Listen to the conversations. Check the foods you hear in each conversation.

1		✓					✓	✓
2								
3								
4								
5								

3 **PAIR WORK** Which foods do you like? Tell your partner. Compare your likes and dislikes.

" I don't like bananas, but I really like apples. "

4 **GRAMMAR** • *How many / Are there any*

Use <u>How many</u> and <u>Are there any</u> with plural nouns.

How many onions **are there**? (Ten or twelve.)
How many apples **are there** in the refrigerator? (I'm not sure. Maybe two.)
Are there any lemons? (Yes, there are. OR Yes. There are three.)
(No, there aren't. OR No. There aren't any.)

80 UNIT 10

5 ▶4:04 **VOCABULARY** • *Places to keep food in a kitchen* Read and listen. Then listen again and repeat.

1 in the fridge (in the refrigerator)   2 on the shelf   3 on the counter

6 **PAIR WORK** Ask and answer questions about the Vocabulary pictures. Use <u>How many</u> and <u>Are there any</u>.

❝ How many potatoes are there on the shelf? ❞

❝ There are three. ❞

NOW YOU CAN Discuss ingredients for a recipe

1 ▶4:05 **CONVERSATION MODEL** Read and listen.

A: How about some green bean salad?
B: Green bean salad? That sounds delicious! I love green beans.
A: Are there any beans in the fridge?
B: Yes, there are.
A: And do we have any onions?
B: I'm not sure. I'll check.

2 ▶4:06 **RHYTHM AND INTONATION** Listen again and repeat. Then practice the Conversation Model with a partner.

3 **CONVERSATION ACTIVATOR** With a partner, change the conversation. Use the recipes. Then change roles. Start like this:

A: How about some ………?
B: ………? That sounds delicious! I love ………..
A: Are there any ………?
B: ………..

Continue with the other ingredients in the recipe.

DON'T STOP!
Talk about what you need, want, have, and like.

RECYCLE THIS LANGUAGE.	
We need [onions].	And how about ___?
We don't have [eggs].	Uh-oh.
I really like [beans].	I don't know.
I don't like [peas].	Sounds nice.

4 **CHANGE PARTNERS** Discuss another recipe.

Green Bean Salad
Ingredients:
beans
peas
onions

Fruit Salad
Ingredients:
apples
bananas
oranges

Tomato Potato Soup
Ingredients:
tomatoes
potatoes
onions

Potato Pancakes
Ingredients:
potatoes
onions
eggs

Stuffed Peppers
Ingredients:
peppers
tomatoes
onions

UNIT 10   81

LESSON 2 — GOAL: Offer and ask for foods

1 ▶ 4:07 **VOCABULARY** • *Drinks and foods: non-count nouns* Read and listen. Then listen again and repeat.

DRINKS
1 water 2 coffee 3 tea 4 juice 5 milk 6 soda

FOODS
7 bread 8 pasta 9 rice 10 cheese 11 meat 12 chicken
13 fish 14 oil 15 butter 16 sugar 17 salt 18 pepper

2 **VOCABULARY PRACTICE** Which foods from the Vocabulary do you like? Discuss with your classmates.

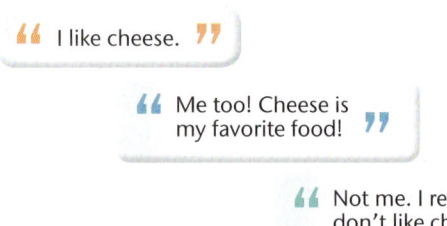

" I like cheese. "

" Me too! Cheese is my favorite food! "

" Not me. I really don't like cheese. "

3 **GRAMMAR** • *Count nouns and non-count nouns*

Count nouns name things you can count. They can be singular or plural.	Non-count nouns name things you cannot count. They are not singular or plural.
I want **an apple**. I like **bananas**. We have **three tomatoes** on the shelf.	I don't eat **sugar**. **Rice** is good for you. **Pasta** is my favorite food.

Be careful!
- Use singular verbs with non-count nouns.
  Rice **is** good for you.
  NOT Rice ~~are~~ good for you.
- Don't use **-s** or **a / an** with non-count nouns.
  rice NOT ~~a rice~~
         NOT ~~two rices~~

82 UNIT 10

4 **GRAMMAR PRACTICE** Complete the chart. Be careful! Make your count nouns plural. But don't make your non-count nouns plural. Then compare with a partner.

I eat	pasta, peas...
I don't eat	
I drink	
I don't drink	

5 **GRAMMAR** • *How much / Is there any*

Use <u>How much</u> and <u>Is there any</u> to ask about non-count nouns.
How much bread does she want? (NOT How many bread does she want?)
How much milk is there? (NOT How many milk is there?)
Is there any butter? Yes, there is. / No, there isn't. OR No. There isn't any.

Remember:
Use <u>How many</u> with plural count nouns.
How many apples are there?
NOT How much apples are there?

6 ▶ 4:08 **VOCABULARY** • *Containers and quantities* Read and listen. Then listen again and repeat.

1 a box of pasta   2 a loaf of bread   3 a bottle of juice   4 a can of soda   5 a bag of onions

7 **GRAMMAR PRACTICE** Complete each question with <u>How much</u> or <u>How many</u>.

1 .... loaves of bread do you need?
2 .... bags of potatoes do we have?
3 .... cheese is there in the fridge?
4 .... sugar do you want in your tea?
5 .... eggs are there for the potato pancakes?
6 .... cans of tomatoes are there on the shelf?

NOW YOU CAN Offer and ask for foods

1 ▶ 4:09 **CONVERSATION MODEL** Read and listen.

A: Would you like coffee or tea?
B: I'd like coffee, please. Thanks.
A: And would you like sugar?
B: No, thanks.
A: Please pass the butter.
B: Here you go.

2 ▶ 4:10 **RHYTHM AND INTONATION** Listen again and repeat. Then practice the Conversation Model with a partner.

3 **CONVERSATION ACTIVATOR** With a partner, change the conversation. Use other foods and drinks. Then change roles.

A: Would you like .... or .... ?
B: I'd like ...., please. Thanks.
A: And would you like .... ?
B: ....
A: Please pass the ....
B: Here you go.

4 **CHANGE PARTNERS** Change the conversation again.

UNIT 10 83

LESSON 3 · GOAL Invite someone to join you at the table

1 GRAMMAR • *The simple present tense and the present continuous*

Remember: Use the simple present tense with verbs have, want, need, and like.
 I **like** coffee. NOT I'm liking coffee.

Use the simple present tense to describe habitual actions and with frequency adverbs.
 I **cook** dinner every day.
 I never **eat** eggs for breakfast.

Use the present continuous for actions in progress right now.
 We**'re making** dinner now.
 She**'s studying** English this year.

Be careful!
Don't say: We cook dinner now.
Don't say: I am cooking dinner every day.

2 GRAMMAR PRACTICE Complete each statement or question with the simple present tense or the present continuous.

1. Who .... lunch in the kitchen right now? *(eat)*
2. Where .... he usually .... lunch—at home or at the office? *(eat)*
3. They .... a lot of sugar in their tea. *(not like)*
4. We .... the kitchen every day. *(clean)*
5. Elaine and Joe aren't here. They .... to work. *(drive)*
6. Why .... six cans of tomatoes? *(you / need)* .... tomato soup for lunch? *(you / make)*
7. .... to work tomorrow? *(she / go)*
8. How many boxes of rice ....? *(he / want)*
9. I .... a bottle of juice in the fridge. *(not have)*
10. I can't talk right now. I .... *(study)*

3 GRAMMAR PRACTICE Look at Suzanne and her weekly schedule. Then write about Suzanne. What is she doing right now? What does she do at other times? Use the present continuous and the simple present tense.

Suzanne is listening to music right now. She teaches English on Mondays, Tuesdays . . .

4 PAIR WORK Ask and answer questions about Suzanne's activities. Use the simple present tense and the present continuous.

" Does Suzanne teach English? "   " Yes, she does. "
" What's Suzanne doing right now? "   " She's listening to music. "

5 ▶ 4:11 **PRONUNCIATION** • *Vowel sounds* Read and listen to the words in each group. Then listen again and repeat.

1 /i/	2 /ɪ/	3 /eɪ/	4 /ɛ/	5 /æ/
see	six	late	pepper	apple
tea	fish	potato	red	jacket
street	this	train	lemon	has

6 **PAIR WORK** Read aloud a word from the Pronunciation chart. Your partner says another word from the same group.

" fish "   " six "

NOW YOU CAN Invite someone to join you at the table

1 ▶ 4:12 **CONVERSATION MODEL** Read and listen.

  A: Hi, Alison. Nice to see you!
  B: You too, Rita. Do you come here often?
  A: Yes, I do. Would you like to join me?
  B: Sure. What are you drinking?
  A: Lemonade.
  B: Mmm. Sounds good.

2 ▶ 4:13 **RHYTHM AND INTONATION** Listen again and repeat. Then practice the Conversation Model with a partner.

3 **CONVERSATION ACTIVATOR** With a partner, personalize the conversation. Use your own name and your own foods or drinks or use the pictures. Then change roles.

  A: Hi, ………. Nice to see you!
  B: You, too, ………. Do you come here often?
  A: Yes, I do. Would you like to join me?
  B: Sure. What are you ………?
  A: ……….
  B: Mmm. Sounds good.

DON'T STOP!
Offer foods and drinks.

  RECYCLE THIS LANGUAGE.
Would you like [coffee]?
Yes, thanks. / No, thanks.

4 **CHANGE PARTNERS** Invite another classmate to join you.

UNIT 10 85

EXTENSION

1 ▶4:14 **READING** Read a recipe with only three ingredients.

▶4:15 **Cooking verbs**

Hungarian Cabbage and Noodles

Ingredients
1 large head of green cabbage
1/2 cup unsalted butter
11 ounces (700 grams) of egg noodles

1. Cut the cabbage into small slices.
2. Put the cabbage into a large bowl and add salt.
3. Put the cabbage into the refrigerator overnight.
4. The next day, drain the cabbage.
5. Melt the butter in a large pan.
6. Sauté the cabbage until it is light brown and very soft (30-40 minutes).
7. Cook the noodles and drain them. Mix them with the cabbage. Add lots of black pepper.

1 cut   2 add
3 put   4 drain
5 melt 6 sauté
7 cook

Source: Adapted from *Recipes 1-2-3* by Rozanne Gold (New York: Viking, 1997)

2 **READING COMPREHENSION** Answer the questions. Compare your answers with a partner.

1 How many ingredients does the recipe have? ....
2 What are the ingredients? ....
3 Is there any butter or oil in the recipe? ....

3 ▶4:16 **LISTENING COMPREHENSION** Listen to the radio cooking program. Write the correct quantity next to each ingredient. Then listen again and number the pictures in the correct order. Listen again and check your work.

Pasta with Garlic and Olive Oil

Ingredients:
__ cloves of garlic
__ tablespoons of olive oil
__ box of pasta

4 **SPEAKING PRACTICE** Tell a partner what you eat for each meal.

"My favorite food for breakfast is eggs."

GRAMMAR BOOSTER
Unit 10 review • p. 142

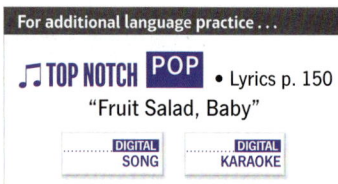

For additional language practice...
🎵 TOP NOTCH POP • Lyrics p. 150
"Fruit Salad, Baby"

REVIEW

Monday / Wednesday / Friday
Michael: do laundry
(Monday only)
Sylvia: go shopping
Sylvia: cook dinner

Tuesday / Thursday / Saturday
Sylvia: take out the garbage
Michael: go shopping and cook dinner

Sunday
No Chores!

Monday

Tuesday

Friday

MEMORY GAME Look at the pictures for one minute. Then close your books and say all the foods and drinks you remember. Use count and non-count nouns correctly.

DESCRIPTION Use the schedule and the pictures to describe Michael and Sylvia's activities and habitual actions. Use the present continuous and the simple present tense. For example:

It's Tuesday. Michael is cooking dinner. Sylvia cooks dinner on Mondays.

PAIR WORK

1 Ask and answer questions about the pictures. Use How many and How much. Answer with There is and There are. For example:
 A: *How many boxes of pasta are there on the counter?*
 B: *There are two.*

2 Create conversations for Michael and Sylvia in the three pictures. For example:
 A: *Would you like peas?*
 B: *Yes, please. And please pass the salt.*

WRITING Write about what you eat on a typical day. Start like this: *For breakfast I eat . . .*

WRITING BOOSTER p. 148
Guidance for this writing exercise

✓ NOW I CAN

☐ Discuss ingredients for a recipe.
☐ Offer and ask for foods.
☐ Invite someone to join me at the table.

UNIT 10   87

COMMUNICATION GOALS

1 Tell someone about an event.
2 Describe your past activities.
3 Talk about your weekend.

UNIT 11 Past Events

LESSON 1 GOAL Tell someone about an event

1 ▶4:19 **VOCABULARY** • ***Describing times before today*** Read and listen. Then listen again and repeat.

1 the day before yesterday	2 yesterday	today
August 30	August 31	September 1

3 last week / month / year / Tuesday — today

4 two days / weeks / months / years ago — today

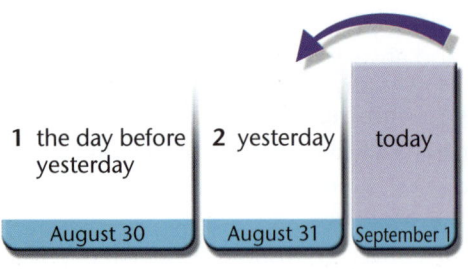

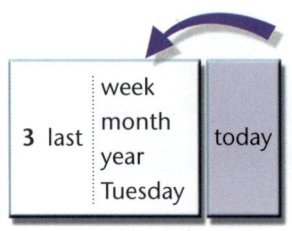

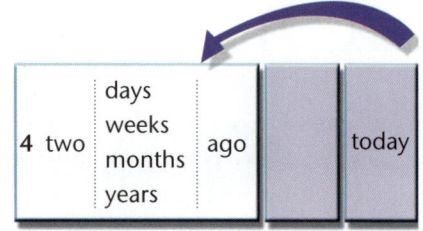

2 ▶4:21 **LISTENING COMPREHENSION** Listen and circle the year.

1 1913 / 1930
2 2016 / 2060
3 1967 / 1976
4 2001 / 2021

▶4:20 **Years, decades, and centuries**

1900 = nineteen hundred
1901 = nineteen oh one
2000 = two thousand
2001 = two thousand one
2010 = twenty ten / two thousand ten
1990 to 1999 = the (nineteen) nineties
1901 to 2000 = the twentieth century
2001 to 2100 = the twenty-first century

3 **PAIR WORK** Choose five of the following years. Say a year to your partner. Your partner circles the year.

2008	1914	1910	1809	1955	1800
1998	1814	1615	2016	1922	2012

4 **GRAMMAR** • ***The past tense of be: statements and questions; there was / there were***

Statements

Singular

I / He / She **was** / **wasn't** at school yesterday.

There was a concert last night.

Plural

We / You / They **were** / **weren't** at home.

There were two movies last weekend.

Contractions

was not → **wasn't**
were not → **weren't**

Questions

Singular

Was it cloudy yesterday?
(Yes, it was. / No, it wasn't.)
Was there a game at the stadium?
(Yes, there was. / No, there wasn't.)

Where **was** the party last night?
When **was** she in Italy?
Who **was** at the party?

Plural

Were you at the party last night?
(Yes, we were. / No, we weren't.)
Were there students at the meeting?
(Yes, there were. / No, there weren't.)

Where **were** they last weekend?
When **were** you at the bookstore?
Who **were** those students?"

5 **GRAMMAR PRACTICE** With a partner, take turns asking and answering the questions about the calendar. Today is April 20.

1 What day was yesterday?
2 What day was six days ago?
3 What day was one month ago?
4 What day was the day before yesterday?
5 What were the dates of last Saturday and Sunday?
6 What day was two months ago?

"Yesterday was April 19th."

APRIL						
Sun	Mon	Tues	Wed	Thurs	Fri	Sat
	1	2	3	4	5	6
7	8	9	10	11	12	13
14	15	16	17	18	19	20
21	22	23	24	25	26	27
28	29	30				

6 ▶ 4:22 **LISTENING COMPREHENSION** Listen to the conversations about events. Then listen again and circle the correct day or month.

1 If today is Sunday, then the party was on (Saturday / Friday / Thursday).
2 If this is January, then their birthdays were in (February / December / January).
3 If today is Friday, then the game was on (Monday / Thursday / Wednesday).

NOW YOU CAN Tell someone about an event

1 ▶ 4:23 **CONVERSATION MODEL** Read and listen.

A: Where were you last night?
B: What time?
A: At about 8:00.
B: I was at home. Why?
A: Because there was a great party at Celia's house.
B: There was? Too bad I wasn't there!

2 ▶ 4:24 **RHYTHM AND INTONATION** Listen again and repeat. Then practice the Conversation Model with a partner.

3 **CONVERSATION ACTIVATOR** Make a list of places for an event in your city or town. Use the pictures for kinds of events. With a partner, change the conversation, using your events. Then change roles.

A: Where were you .... ?
B: What time?
A: At about ....
B: I was at .... Why?
A: Because there was a .... at ....
B: There was? Too bad I wasn't there!

4 **CHANGE PARTNERS** Talk about other events and places.

LESSON 2 GOAL Describe your past activities

1 GRAMMAR • *The simple past tense: statements*

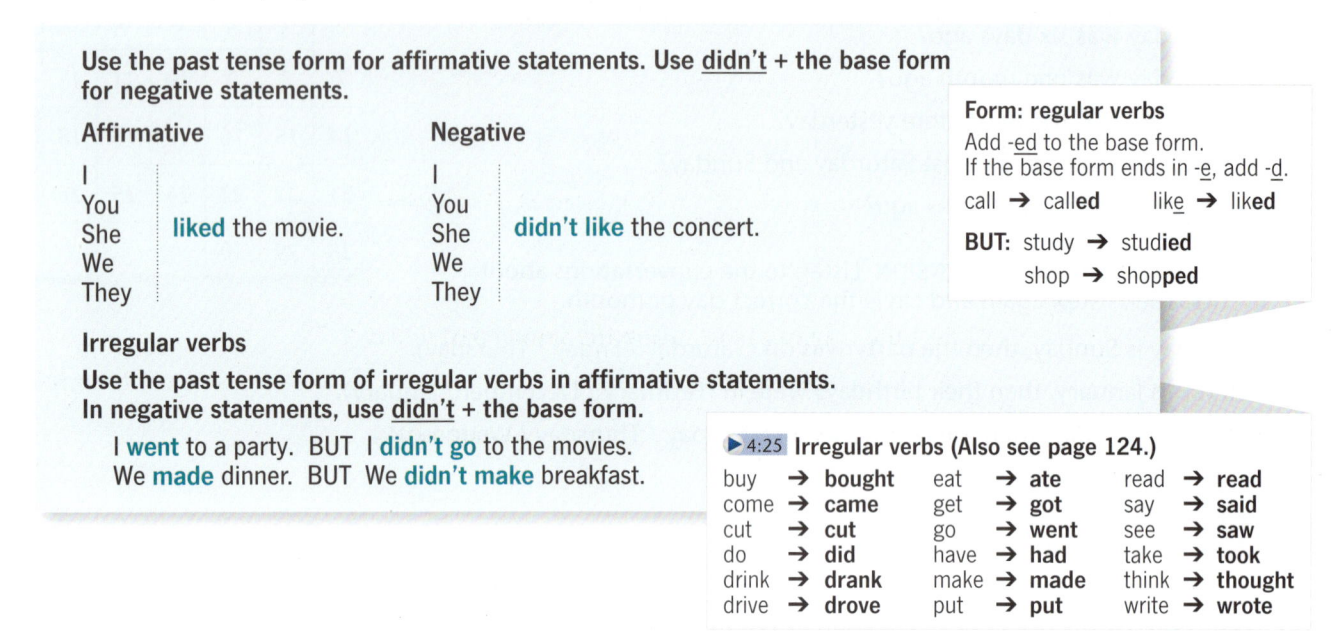

Use the past tense form for affirmative statements. Use <u>didn't</u> + the base form for negative statements.

Affirmative

I
You
She   liked the movie.
We
They

Negative

I
You
She   didn't like the concert.
We
They

Form: regular verbs
Add -ed to the base form.
If the base form ends in -e, add -d.
call → call**ed**   like → lik**ed**
BUT: study → stud**ied**
        shop → shop**ped**

Irregular verbs

Use the past tense form of irregular verbs in affirmative statements.
In negative statements, use <u>didn't</u> + the base form.

I **went** to a party. BUT I **didn't go** to the movies.
We **made** dinner. BUT We **didn't make** breakfast.

▶ 4:25 Irregular verbs (Also see page 124.)

buy → bought	eat → ate	read → read
come → came	get → got	say → said
cut → cut	go → went	see → saw
do → did	have → had	take → took
drink → drank	make → made	think → thought
drive → drove	put → put	write → wrote

2 ▶ 4:26 PRONUNCIATION • *The regular simple past tense ending* Listen. Then listen again and repeat.

1 /d/	2 /t/	3 /ɪd/
listened = listen/d/	liked = like/t/	wanted = want/ɪd/
exercised = exercise/d/	washed = wash/t/	needed = need/ɪd/

3 GRAMMAR PRACTICE Complete the e-mail. Use the simple past tense and the past tense of <u>be</u>.

< INBOX (12)

Hi, Lucille: Yesterday was a really nice day. I .... early, ... my teeth,
                                                                  1 get up   2 brush
.... breakfast, and .... my house—all before 8:30. Then I ....
   3 make   4 clean   5 work
until noon. After lunch, I .... to the weather report, and the weather ....
                              6 listen   7 be
warm. I .... all my grandchildren here. They .... here in the afternoon.
            8 invite   9 come
We .... together for a while, and then the younger children .... a nap.
      10 talk   11 take
The older ones .... to the park and .... soccer. At the end of the day, I
                      12 go   13 play
.... dinner for all the children. They .... the dinner because it was pasta.
  14 cook   15 love
The kids .... everything and .... more! Great day!
              16 eat   17 want
Brian

90   UNIT 11

4 GRAMMAR • *The simple past tense: questions*

Question forms are the same with regular and irregular verbs.

Did	I / you / he / she / we / they	watch TV last night? see a movie?	Yes, No,	I / you / he / she / we / they	did. didn't.

Where **did** you **go** last weekend?
What time **did** they **go** out to dinner?
What **did** your friend **watch** on TV?
How many cups of coffee **did** she **drink**?
Who **did** they **see** yesterday?

Be careful!
Remember: Word order changes when **Who** is the subject of the sentence:
Who went to the mall this morning? (We did.)

5 GRAMMAR PRACTICE Complete the conversations, using the simple past tense.

1 A: Where .... on Saturday?
        1 your family / go
   B: .... to the movies. .... a
        2 We / go   *3 we / see*
   good family movie.
   A: .... out to eat afterwards?
        4 you / go
   B: Yes, we ....
                5   *6 We / eat*
   Indonesian food. .... a lot of pepper.
                        7 It / have
   A: But ....
            8 I / think   *9 your husband / not like*
   peppery food.
   B: Actually, ... a little and
                    10 he / eat
   .... it was good.
      11 he / say

2 A: .... out the garbage this morning?
        12 who / take
   B: Actually, Laura ....
                        13
   A: And .... the laundry?
            14 who / do
   B: I'm not sure. But I think .... the
                                    15 Laura / do
   laundry this morning, too.
   A: That's great, but .... any household
                        16 you / do
   chores?
   B: Me? Last week .... all the chores:
                        17 I / do
   .... shopping, and .... home
      18 I / go   *19 I / come*
   early, and .... dinner every night.
                20 I / make

NOW YOU CAN Describe your past activities

1 ▶4:27 **CONVERSATION MODEL** Read and listen.

   A: So what did you do yesterday?
   B: Well, I got up at seven, I made breakfast, and then I went to work.
   A: What about after work? Did you do anything special?
   B: Not really. I just made dinner and watched a movie.

2 ▶4:28 **RHYTHM AND INTONATION** Listen again and repeat. Then practice the Conversation Model with a partner.

3 **CONVERSATION ACTIVATOR** With a partner, personalize the conversation. Describe your past activities. Then change roles.

   A: So what did you do .... ?
   B: Well, I .... , and then I ....
   A: What about .... ? Did you do anything special?
   B: ....

DON'T STOP!
Ask more questions.
Did you [wash the dishes]?
Who [took out the garbage]?
When did you [go to the movies]?

4 **CHANGE PARTNERS** Ask about other past activities.

Ideas
- household chores
- leisure activities
- entertainment events

LESSON 3 **GOAL** Talk about your weekend

1 ▶4:29 **VOCABULARY** • *Outdoor activities* Read and listen. Then listen again and repeat.

VOCABULARY BOOSTER
More outdoor activities • p. 132

1 go to the beach

2 go running

3 go bike riding

4 go for a walk

5 go swimming

6 go for a drive

2 **PAIR WORK** Ask and answer questions with <u>When</u> and <u>How often</u> and the Vocabulary. Use the simple present tense.

" How often do you go to the beach? "

" I go about once a month. "

3 ▶4:30 **LISTENING COMPREHENSION** Listen to the conversations. Then check the correct picture to complete each statement.

1 Rosalie went ___.
a   b

2 She's going ___.
a   b

3 They're going ___.
a   b

4 He went ___.
a   b

NOW YOU CAN Talk about your weekend

1. ▶ 4:31 **CONVERSATION MODEL** Read and listen.

   A: Did you have a good weekend?
   B: Let me think. . . . Oh, yeah. I had a great weekend.
   A: What did you do?
   B: Well, on Saturday, my friends and I went bike riding and to a movie. Then on Sunday, I went for a drive. What about you?
   A: Well, on Saturday, the weather was great, so I went for a walk. And on Sunday, my family and I went to the beach.

2. ▶ 4:32 **RHYTHM AND INTONATION** Listen again and repeat. Then practice the Conversation Model with a partner.

3. **NOTEPADDING** On the notepad, write what you did on the weekend.

On Saturday

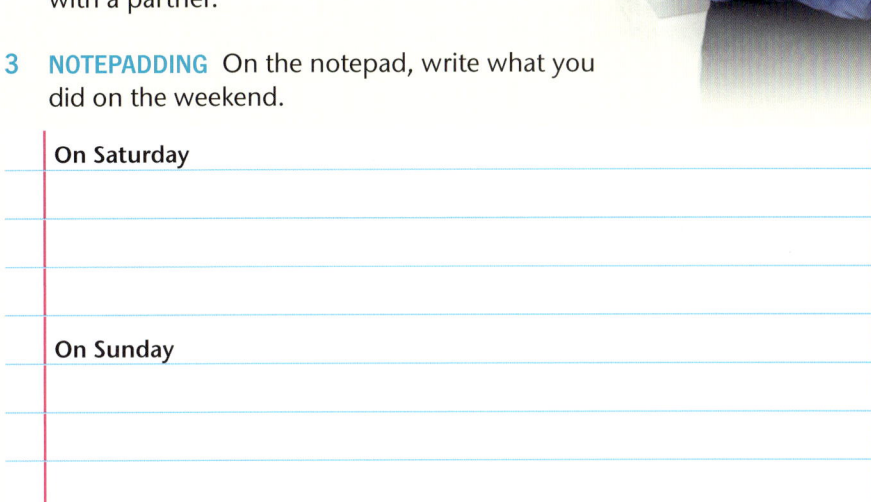

On Sunday

4. **CONVERSATION ACTIVATOR** With a partner, personalize the conversation. Use your own information and the simple past tense.

   A: Did you have a good weekend?
   B: Let me think . . . Oh, yeah. I ....
   A: What did you do?
   B: Well, ... Then .... What about you?
   A: Well, on ...., the weather was ...., so I .... And on Sunday, ...

5. **CHANGE PARTNERS** Talk about more weekend activities.

DON'T STOP!
Ask your partner more questions.

🔁 **RECYCLE THIS LANGUAGE.**
Really?
Did you do anything special?
What time did you come home?
Is [the beach] far from here?
Do you [go swimming] often?
How often do you [go bike riding]?

EXTENSION

1 ▶ 4:33 **READING** Read about what people did last weekend.

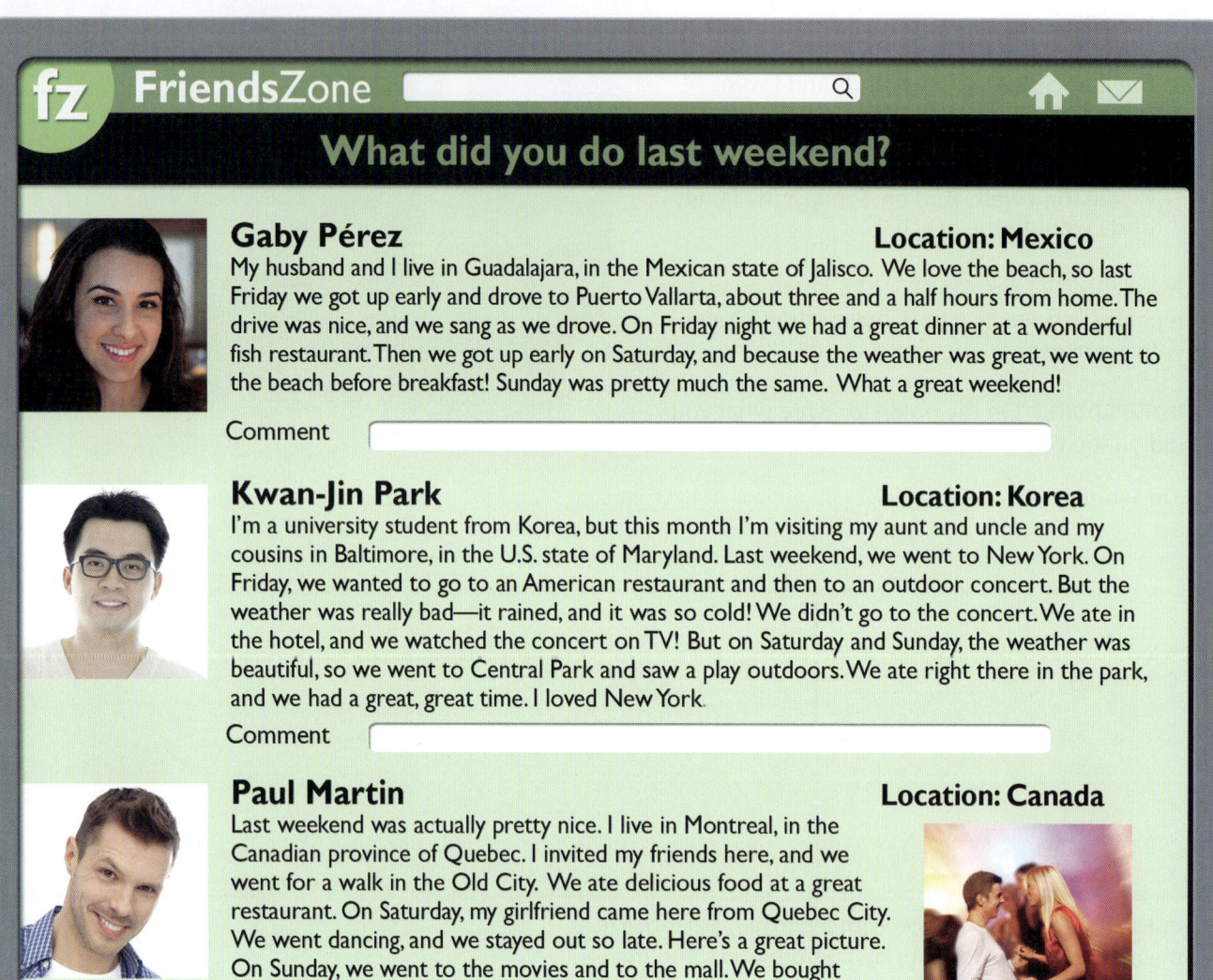

FriendsZone

What did you do last weekend?

Gaby Pérez **Location: Mexico**

My husband and I live in Guadalajara, in the Mexican state of Jalisco. We love the beach, so last Friday we got up early and drove to Puerto Vallarta, about three and a half hours from home. The drive was nice, and we sang as we drove. On Friday night we had a great dinner at a wonderful fish restaurant. Then we got up early on Saturday, and because the weather was great, we went to the beach before breakfast! Sunday was pretty much the same. What a great weekend!

Comment

Kwan-Jin Park **Location: Korea**

I'm a university student from Korea, but this month I'm visiting my aunt and uncle and my cousins in Baltimore, in the U.S. state of Maryland. Last weekend, we went to New York. On Friday, we wanted to go to an American restaurant and then to an outdoor concert. But the weather was really bad—it rained, and it was so cold! We didn't go to the concert. We ate in the hotel, and we watched the concert on TV! But on Saturday and Sunday, the weather was beautiful, so we went to Central Park and saw a play outdoors. We ate right there in the park, and we had a great, great time. I loved New York.

Comment

Paul Martin **Location: Canada**

Last weekend was actually pretty nice. I live in Montreal, in the Canadian province of Quebec. I invited my friends here, and we went for a walk in the Old City. We ate delicious food at a great restaurant. On Saturday, my girlfriend came here from Quebec City. We went dancing, and we stayed out so late. Here's a great picture. On Sunday, we went to the movies and to the mall. We bought new clothes. Montreal has some wonderful stores.

Comment

2 **READING COMPREHENSION** Write one yes / no question and one information question about Gaby, Kwan-Jin, and Paul. Then answer a partner's questions.

	Yes / no questions	Information questions
Gaby		
Kwan-Jin		
Paul		

Ideas
Was [Gaby] in . . .
Did [Kwan-Jin] . . .
Where was ___ . . .   last weekend?
Where did ___ . . .   last Sunday?
What did ___ . . .   on Saturday?
Who was with ___ . . . on Friday night?
When did ___ . . .
What did ___ . . .

3 **SPEAKING / GRAMMAR PRACTICE** Ask your partner questions about an activity in the past. Then tell your classmates about the activity. Use past-time expressions.

GRAMMAR BOOSTER
Unit 11 review • p. 143

For additional language practice . . .
♪ **TOP NOTCH POP** • Lyrics p. 150
"My Favorite Day"
DIGITAL SONG DIGITAL KARAOKE

REVIEW

VERB GAME Form two teams. Look at the pictures for one minute. Then close your books. Each team makes a list of all the actions in the pictures. The team with the most actions wins. For example:

watch TV   do the laundry

STORY Tell a story about one of the people. Use past-time expressions. For example:

Last weekend, Karen went to a concert with her friends. She . . .

PAIR WORK With a partner, play the role of Don or Karen. Discuss your activities from the day before and the weekend before. Start like this:

So what did you do [last weekend] . . . ?

WRITING Choose one of the following topics:
a Write about Don and Karen. Write about what they did.
b Write about your weekend. Write about what you did.

For example: *Last weekend I went to the beach . . .*

WRITING BOOSTER p. 149
Guidance for this writing exercise

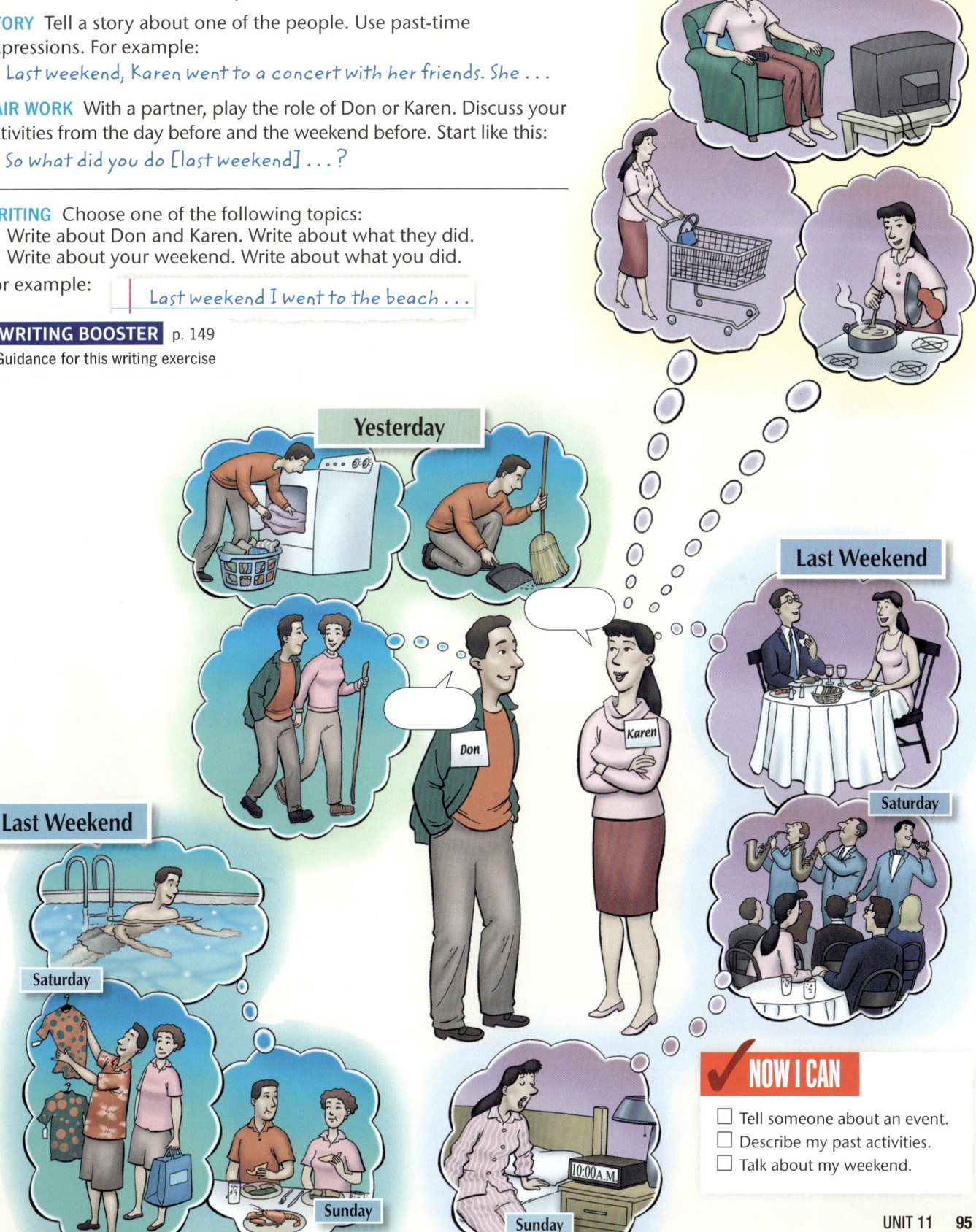

NOW I CAN
☐ Tell someone about an event.
☐ Describe my past activities.
☐ Talk about my weekend.

UNIT 11   95

UNIT 12 Appearance and Health

COMMUNICATION GOALS
1 Describe appearance.
2 Show concern about an injury.
3 Suggest a remedy.

LESSON 1 GOAL Describe appearance

1 ▶ 4:36 **VOCABULARY** • *Adjectives to describe hair* Read and listen. Then listen again and repeat.

1 black   2 brown   3 red   4 blonde   5 gray   6 white

7 dark ← → 8 light

9 straight   10 wavy   11 curly   12 long   13 short

14 He's **bald**.
15 He has a **mustache**.
16 He has a **beard**.
17 He wears **glasses**.

2 ▶ 4:37 **VOCABULARY** • *The face* Read and listen. Then listen again and repeat.

1 eye
2 eyebrow
3 eyelashes
4 nose
5 ear
6 mouth
7 teeth
8 chin

9 brown eyes
10 blue eyes
11 green eyes

two **teeth** BUT one **tooth**

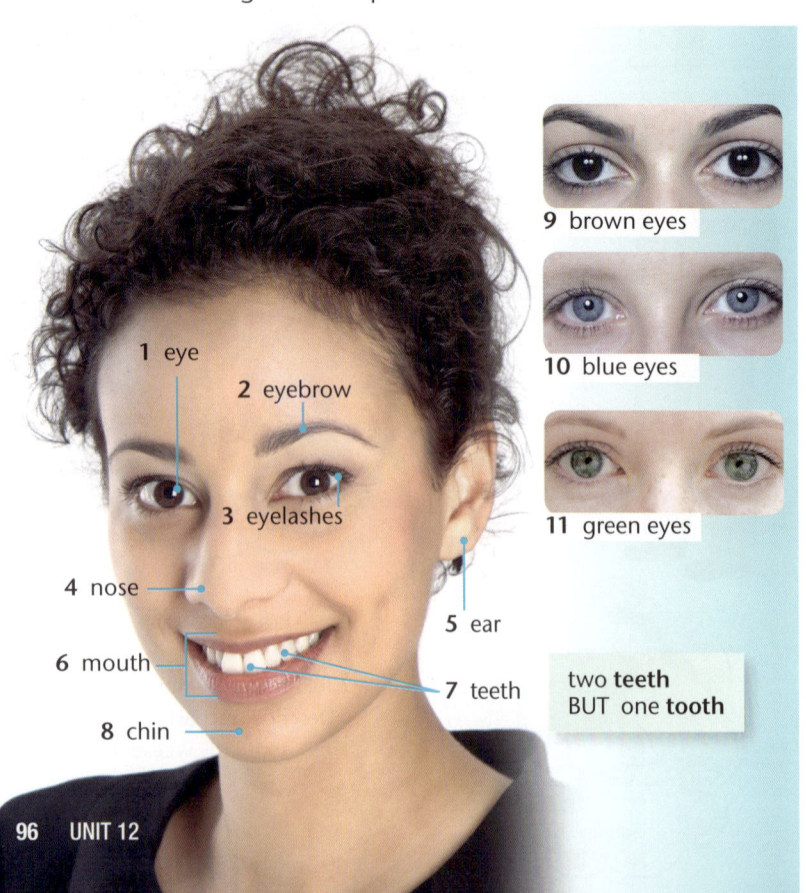

3 ▶ 4:38 **LISTENING COMPREHENSION** Listen to the descriptions. Write the number of the conversation in the circle.

96   UNIT 12

4 GRAMMAR • Describing people with be and have

With be
Her eyes are blue.
Their hair is gray.
Her eyelashes are long and dark.

With have
She has blue eyes.
They have gray hair.
She has long, dark eyelashes.

Remember:
Adjectives come before the nouns they describe.
She has blue eyes. NOT She has eyes blue.
Adjectives are never plural.
She has blue eyes. NOT She has blues eyes.
Her eyes are blue. NOT Her eyes are blues.

5 GRAMMAR PRACTICE Complete each sentence with the correct form of be or have.

1 **A:** What does your brother look like?
  B: Well, he .... a mustache and wavy hair. And he wears glasses.

2 **A:** What does your mother look like?
  B: Her hair .... curly and black.

3 **A:** What does her father look like?
  B: He .... a short, gray beard.

4 **A:** What does his grandmother look like?
  B: She .... curly, gray hair and beautiful eyes.

5 **A:** What does his sister look like?
  B: His sister? Her hair .... long and pretty!

6 **A:** What do your brothers look like?
  B: They .... straight, black hair, and they wear glasses.

NOW YOU CAN Describe appearance

1 ▶ 4:39 **CONVERSATION MODEL** Read and listen.
  A: Who's that? She looks familiar.
  B: Who?
  A: The woman with the long, dark hair.
  B: Oh, that's Ivete Sangalo. She's a singer from Brazil.
  A: No kidding!

2 ▶ 4:40 **RHYTHM AND INTONATION** Listen again and repeat. Then practice the Conversation Model with a partner.

3 **CONVERSATION ACTIVATOR** With a partner, change the conversation. Talk about the people in the photos. (OR use your own photos.) Then change roles.

  A: Who's that? .... looks familiar.
  B: Who?
  A: The .... with the ....
  B: Oh, that's .... 's .... from ....
  A: No kidding!

DON'T STOP!
Say more about the person's appearance.

RECYCLE THIS LANGUAGE.
He's so [good-looking / handsome / old].
She's very [pretty / young / tall].
Her hair is so [wavy / pretty / short].
His eyes are very [blue / dark].

Ivete Sangalo
singer (Brazil)

Andrea Bocelli
singer (Italy)

Amy Adams
actor (U.S.)

Emeli Sandé
singer (U.K.)

Chris Hemsworth
actor (Australia)

4 **CHANGE PARTNERS** Talk about other people.

LESSON 2

GOAL Show concern about an injury

1 ▶ 4:41 **VOCABULARY** • *Parts of the body* Read and listen. Then listen again and repeat.

1 head
2 chest
3 stomach
4 hip
5 knee
6 ankle
7 neck
8 shoulder
9 back
10 arm
11 leg
12 hand
13 finger
14 fingernail
15 foot
16 toe
17 toenail

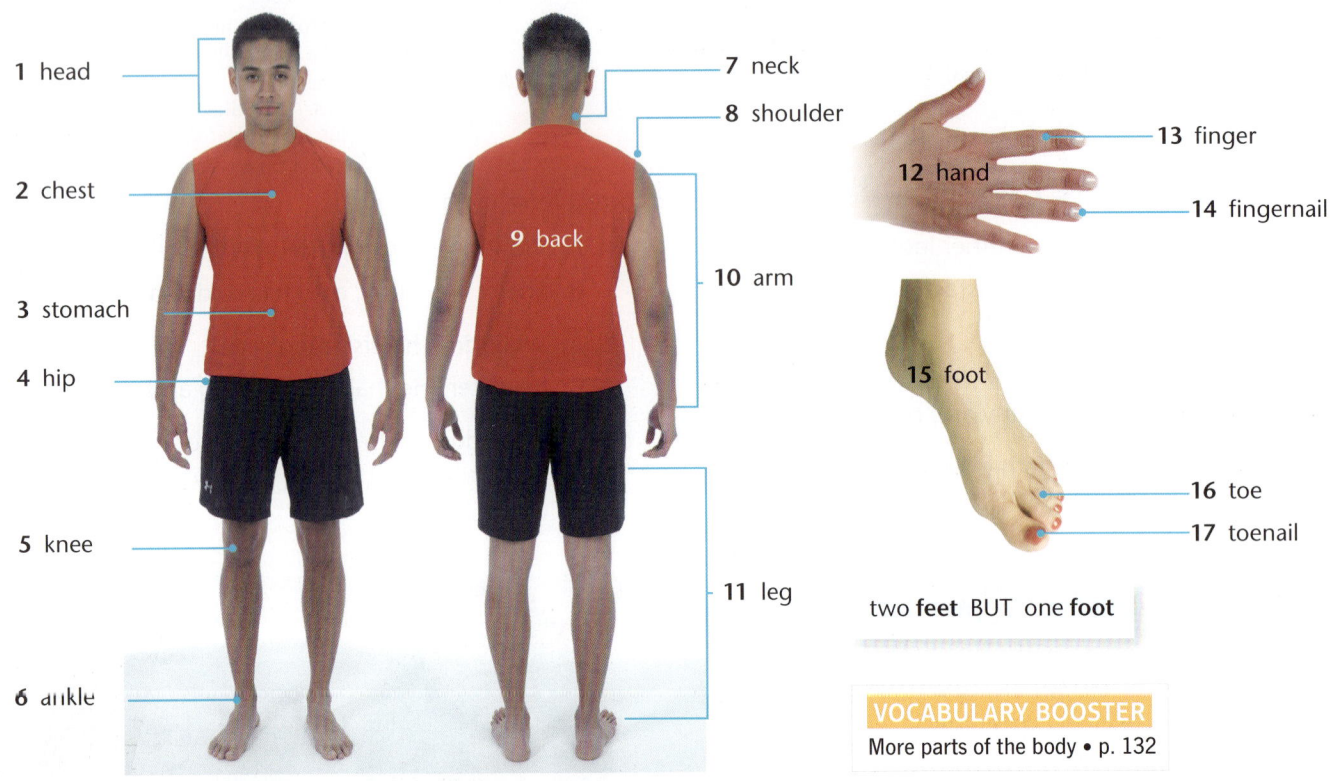

two **feet** BUT one **foot**

VOCABULARY BOOSTER
More parts of the body • p. 132

2 **GAME / VOCABULARY PRACTICE** Follow a classmate's directions. If you make a mistake, sit down.

Touch your toes.

▶ 4:43
base form	past form
burn	burned
hurt	hurt
cut	cut
break	broke
fall	fell

3 ▶ 4:42 **VOCABULARY** • *Accidents and injuries* Read and listen. Then listen again and repeat.

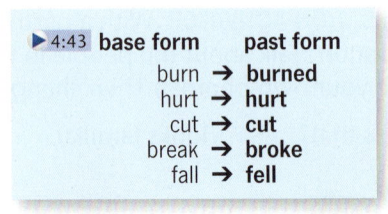

1 He **burned** his finger.
2 She **hurt** her back. 
3 She **cut** her hand. 
4 He **broke** his arm. 
5 He **fell** down.

4 ▶4:44 **LISTENING COMPREHENSION** Listen to the conversations. Write each injury. Then listen again and check your work.

1 She *burned her arm* .
2 He ....
3 She ....
4 He ....
5 She ....
6 He ....

5 ▶4:45 **PRONUNCIATION • More vowel sounds** Read and listen. Then listen again and repeat. Then practice saying the words on your own.

1 /u/	2 /ʊ/	3 /oʊ/	4 /ɔ/	5 /ɑ/
tooth	should	nose	awful	blonde
blue	good	toe	fall	hot
food	foot	broke	long	wash

NOW YOU CAN Show concern about an injury

1 ▶4:46 **CONVERSATION MODEL** Read and listen.

A: Hey, Evan. What happened?
B: I broke my ankle.
A: I'm sorry to hear that. Does it hurt a lot?
B: Actually, no. It doesn't.

▶4:48
Ways to express concern
I'm sorry to hear that.
Oh, no.
That's too bad.

2 ▶4:47 **RHYTHM AND INTONATION** Listen again and repeat. Then practice the Conversation Model with a partner.

3 **CONVERSATION ACTIVATOR** With a partner, change the conversation. Use the pictures for ideas. Then change roles.

A: Hey, ... What happened?
B: I ....
A: .... Does it hurt a lot?
B: Actually, ... It ....

4 **CHANGE PARTNERS** Discuss other injuries.

UNIT 12 99

LESSON 3 — GOAL: Suggest a remedy

1 ▶ 4:49 **VOCABULARY • Ailments** Read and listen. Then listen again and repeat.

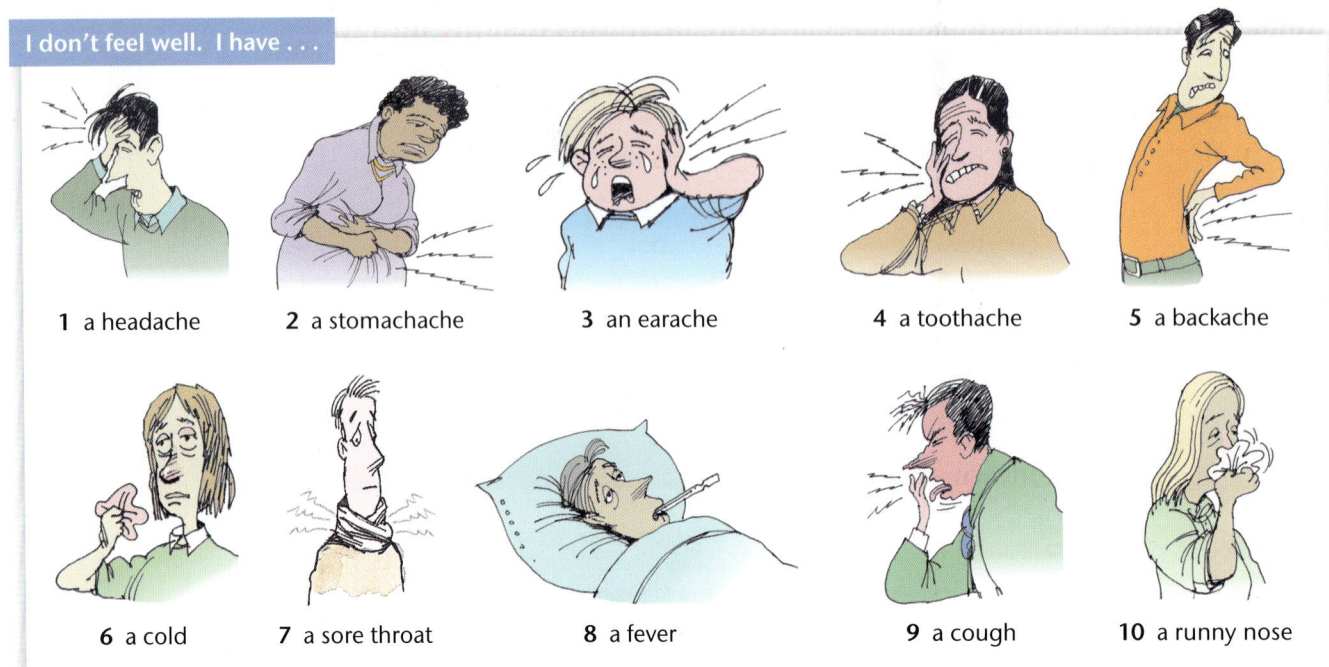

I don't feel well. I have . . .

1. a headache
2. a stomachache
3. an earache
4. a toothache
5. a backache
6. a cold
7. a sore throat
8. a fever
9. a cough
10. a runny nose

2 VOCABULARY PRACTICE Tell your partner about a time you had an ailment. Use the Vocabulary.

"I had a headache last week."

"Really? I never have headaches."

3 ▶ 4:50 **VOCABULARY • Remedies** Read and listen. Then listen again and repeat.

1. take something
2. lie down 
3. have some tea 
4. see a doctor / see a dentist 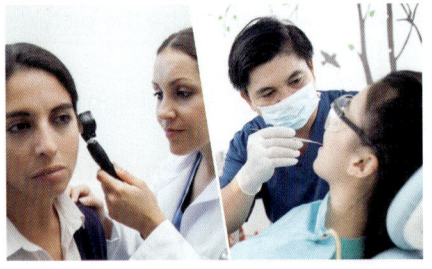

4 GRAMMAR • Should + base form for suggestions

Use should with the base form of a verb.

| I / You / He / She / We / They | **should take** something. **shouldn't go** to work. |

You **should see** a doctor.

He **shouldn't go** to school today.

100 UNIT 12

5 ▶4:51 **LISTENING COMPREHENSION** Listen to the conversations. Check the correct ailments. Then complete the suggestion for a remedy each person gives. Use should.

	a cold	a fever	a headache	a stomachache	a sore throat	a backache	a toothache	Remedy
1	☐	☐	☐	☐	☐	☐	☐	She *should take something.*
2	☐	☐	☐	☐	☐	☐	☐	He
3	☐	☐	☐	☐	☐	☐	☐	She
4	☐	☐	☐	☐	☐	☐	☐	He
5	☐	☐	☐	☐	☐	☐	☐	She
6	☐	☐	☐	☐	☐	☐	☐	He

6 **VOCABULARY / GRAMMAR PRACTICE** Work with a partner. Listen to your partner's ailments. Suggest remedies. Use should or shouldn't.

Partner A's ailments
1 I have a backache.
2 I don't feel well. I think I have a fever.
3 My son doesn't feel well. He has a cough.

Partner B's ailments
1 I have a bad toothache.
2 I have a sore throat.
3 My wife feels really bad. She has a stomachache.

NOW YOU CAN Suggest a remedy

1 ▶4:52 **CONVERSATION MODEL** Read and listen.

A: I don't feel well.
B: What's wrong?
A: I have a headache.
B: Oh, that's too bad. You really should take something.
A: Good idea. Thanks.
B: I hope you feel better.

▶4:54
Ways to say you're sick
I don't feel well.
I feel terrible.
I don't feel so good.

2 ▶4:53 **RHYTHM AND INTONATION** Listen again and repeat. Then practice the Conversation Model with a partner.

3 **CONVERSATION ACTIVATOR** With a partner, change the conversation. Suggest a remedy with should. Then change roles.

A: ....
B: What's wrong?
A: ....
B: .... You really ....
A: .... Thanks.
B: I hope you feel better.

DON'T STOP!
Give other advice, using should or shouldn't.
Ideas
✓ go to bed   ✗ go to class
✓ take a nap   ✗ exercise

4 **CHANGE PARTNERS** Discuss other ailments.

EXTENSION

1 ▶ 4:55 **READING** Look at the photos and read the descriptions. Do you know these famous people?

Johnny Depp

John Christopher Depp is an actor from the U.S., famous as "Johnny Depp." Depp's father was an engineer, and his mother worked in a restaurant. Before he was an actor, he was a rock musician. On a trip to Los Angeles, he met the actor Nicholas Cage. Cage gave Depp some advice: he should be an actor. Today, Depp is famous around the world for his movies. He changes his style a lot for different movie parts. Sometimes his hair is short. Sometimes he wears glasses and has long hair. And sometimes he doesn't shave and has a mustache and a beard. Many people think he is very handsome—and a very good actor. Depp has two children, Lily-Rose and Jack.

Shakira

Shakira Isabel Mebarak Ripoll is a singer and songwriter from Barranquilla, Colombia. Her father's family came from Lebanon, so she often listened and danced to traditional Arab music. In 1996 Shakira's Spanish-language album Pies Descalzos made her famous all over Latin America and Spain, and she became a star. In 2001, she recorded her first songs in English on the album Laundry Service. Today, Shakira is a TV star too, and she is famous all over the world. When Shakira was young, she had long black hair. Later, she changed her hair style to long and blonde. But her fans think she is beautiful in any style.

2 **READING COMPREHENSION** Answer the questions. Write the person.

| Johnny Depp | Depp's father | Shakira | Nicholas Cage |
| Depp's children | Depp's mother | Shakira's grandparents | |

1 Who acts in movies? ....
2 Who is a grandmother? ....
3 Who is from Lebanon? ....
4 Whose father was a musician? ....
5 Who gave good advice? ....
6 Who was an engineer? ....

3 **PAIR WORK** Partner A describes Shakira in her two pictures. Partner B describes Johnny Depp in his two pictures. Which pictures do you like?

" I like Shakira in the first picture. She has... "

4 **DISCUSSION** What kind of hair is good-looking for women? What kind of hair is good-looking for men?

" I like short, wavy hair on men. "

5 **GROUP WORK** Describe someone in your class. Your classmates guess who it is.

" She's short and very good-looking. She has long hair and brown eyes. She's wearing a white blouse and a blue skirt. "

GRAMMAR BOOSTER
Unit 12 review • p. 143

REVIEW

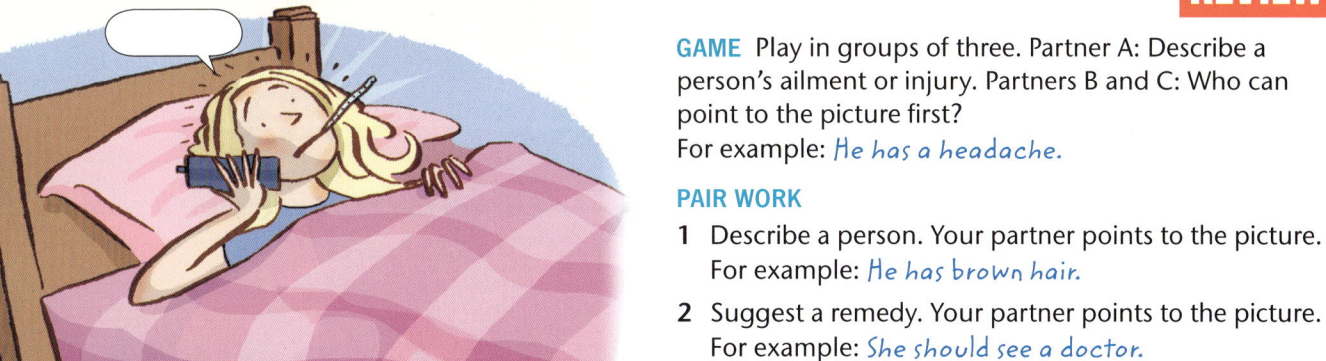

GAME Play in groups of three. Partner A: Describe a person's ailment or injury. Partners B and C: Who can point to the picture first?
For example: *He has a headache.*

PAIR WORK

1 Describe a person. Your partner points to the picture. For example: *He has brown hair.*

2 Suggest a remedy. Your partner points to the picture. For example: *She should see a doctor.*

3 Create a conversation for each situation. Start like this: *What happened?* OR *I feel terrible.*

WRITING Describe someone you know. Use the vocabulary from this unit and from Unit 4. For example:

My friend Sam is very handsome.
He has short, curly hair . . .

WRITING BOOSTER p. 149
Guidance for this writing exercise

✓ NOW I CAN
☐ Describe appearance.
☐ Show concern about an injury.
☐ Suggest a remedy.

UNIT 12

UNIT 13 Abilities and Requests

COMMUNICATION GOALS
1. Discuss your abilities.
2. Politely decline an invitation.
3. Ask for and agree to do a favor.

LESSON 1

GOAL Discuss your abilities

1 ▶ 5:02 **VOCABULARY • Abilities** Read and listen. Then listen again and repeat.

VOCABULARY BOOSTER
More musical instruments • p. 133

1 sing
2 dance 
3 swim 
4 play the guitar / the violin 
5 ski 
6 cook 
7 sew 
8 knit 
9 draw 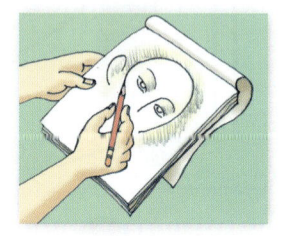
10 paint 
11 drive 
12 fix things 

▶ 5:03 **Adverbs well and badly**

Tom **sings well**.   Ryan **sings badly**.

2 VOCABULARY PRACTICE Write three things you do well and three things you do badly.

1 I sing well.	1 I dance badly.
1	1
2	2
3	3

3 PAIR WORK Tell your partner about your abilities. Use your sentences from Vocabulary Practice with <u>and</u> and <u>but</u>.

" I sing well, **but** I dance badly. "

" I draw well, **and** I paint well, too. "

4 GROUP WORK Tell your class about some of your partner's abilities.

" Ann sings well, **but** she dances badly. She plays the guitar, **and** she plays the violin, too. "

5 GRAMMAR • Can and can't for ability

To talk about ability, use can or can't and the base form of a verb.

Carrie can play the guitar.   Josie can't cook.

Questions
Can you play the guitar?
Can he speak English?

Short answers
Yes, I can. / No, I can't.
Yes, he can. / No, he can't.

Use can or can't with well to indicate degree of ability.
She can play the guitar, but she can't play well.

can't = can not = cannot

6 GRAMMAR PRACTICE Complete each conversation with can or can't and the base form of a verb.

1 A: .... you .... the guitar?
   B: Yes, I .... But I don't play well.

2 A: .... Gwen .... well?
   B: Yes, she .... She swims very well.

3 A: .... your brother ....?
   B: My brother? No. He .... cook at all.

4 A: .... Gloria .... English well?
   B: No, she .... She needs this class.

5 A: .... your mother ....?
   B: Yes. She knits very well.

6 A: .... your sisters ....?
   B: Yes. They go skiing every weekend.

NOW YOU CAN Discuss your abilities

1 ▶5:04 **CONVERSATION MODEL** Read and listen.

   A: Can you draw?
   B: Actually, yes, I can. Can you?
   A: No, I can't.
   B: Really? That's too bad.

   ▶5:06 **Ways to respond**
   A: I can draw. | A: I can't draw.
   B: That's great! | B: That's too bad.

2 ▶5:05 **RHYTHM AND INTONATION** Listen again and repeat. Then practice the Conversation Model with a partner.

3 **CONVERSATION ACTIVATOR** With a partner, personalize the conversation. Discuss your abilities. Then change roles.

   A: Can you ....?
   B: Actually, ... , I .... Can you?
   A: .... , I ....
   B: Really? That's ....

   DON'T STOP!
   Ask more questions. Say more about your abilities.

4 **CHANGE PARTNERS** Discuss other abilities.

RECYCLE THIS LANGUAGE.

What do you [draw]?   I draw [people].
How often do you [ski]?   I ski [every weekend].
Where do you [sing]?   I sing [in the shower].

LESSON 2 — GOAL: Politely decline an invitation

1 ▶ 5:07 **VOCABULARY • Reasons for not doing something** Read and listen. Then listen again and repeat.

1 She's busy.
2 They're not hungry. 
3 She's full. 
4 He's tired. 
5 It's early. 
6 It's late. 

2 **PAIR WORK** Tell your partner about a time you were busy, tired, or full.

" Last week, I worked late every day. I was so tired. "

3 **GRAMMAR •** *Too* + *adjective*

Too makes an adjective stronger. It usually gives it a negative meaning.
I'm **too busy**. I can't talk right now.
I'm **too tired**. Let's not go to the movies.
It's **too late**. I should go to bed.

Be careful!
Don't use **too** with a positive adjective.
She's so pretty!
NOT She's too pretty!

4 **GRAMMAR PRACTICE** Complete each sentence. Use *too* and an adjective.

1 I don't want these shoes. They're ....
2 It's .... today. She can't go swimming. 
3 I'm .... I can't read right now. 
4 He doesn't want that shirt. It's .... 
5 I can't talk right now. I'm .... 
6 It's .... for a movie. We should go to bed. 

106 UNIT 13

NOW YOU CAN Politely decline an invitation

1 ▶ 5:08 **CONVERSATION MODEL** Read and listen.

   A: Hey, Sue. Let's go to a movie.
   B: I'm really sorry, Paul, but I'm too busy.
   A: That's OK. Maybe some other time.

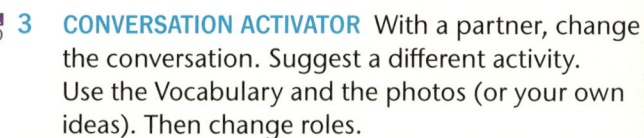

2 ▶ 5:09 **RHYTHM AND INTONATION** Listen again and repeat. Then practice the Conversation Model with a partner.

3 **CONVERSATION ACTIVATOR** With a partner, change the conversation. Suggest a different activity. Use the Vocabulary and the photos (or your own ideas). Then change roles.

   A: Hey, ………. Let's go ……….
   B: I'm really sorry, ………, but ……….
   A: That's OK. Maybe some other time.

   DON'T STOP!
   Suggest another day or time.

   RECYCLE THIS LANGUAGE.
   How about [tomorrow / this weekend / this evening / at 6:00]?
   Sounds great! / OK!
   I'm not hungry.
   I'm too [tired / busy / full].
   It's too [early / late].
   It's too [windy / hot / cold / rainy] today.

4 **CHANGE PARTNERS** Suggest other activities and give other reasons.

LESSON 3

GOAL Ask for and agree to do a favor

1 GRAMMAR • Polite requests with Could you + base form

Use **Could you** and the base form of a verb to make a request.
   Could you wash the dishes?

Use **please** to make a request more polite.
   Could you **please** wash the dishes?

2 ▶ 5:10 VOCABULARY • Favors   Read and listen. Then listen again and repeat.

1 Could you please **help me**?

2 Could you please **open** the window?
Also: open the door / refrigerator 

3 Could you please **close** the door? 
Also: close the window / microwave

4 Could you please **turn on** the light? 
Also: turn on the stove / computer

5 Could you please **turn off** the TV? 
Also: turn off the microwave / light

6 Could you please **hand me** my glasses? 
Also: hand me my sweater / book

3 VOCABULARY / GRAMMAR PRACTICE   Complete the polite requests. Use **Could you please**. Use the Vocabulary and other verbs you know.

1 It's a little hot in here. *Could you please open* .... the window?
2 I have a headache. .... the TV?
3 .... my jacket? I'm going for a walk.
4 I'm going to bed. .... the computer?
5 I want to read a book. .... my glasses?
6 .... shopping? We need milk.
7 I'm busy right now. .... the garbage?
8 Let's watch a movie. .... the TV?

108   UNIT 13

4 ▶5:11 **LISTENING COMPREHENSION** Listen to the conversations. Then complete each request.
1 Could you *close the window* ...., please?
2 Could you ....?
3 Could you please ....?
4 Could you please ....?
5 Could you ....?

5 ▶5:12 **PRONUNCIATION** • **Blending of sounds: Could you . . .** Read and listen. Then listen again and repeat.

/ˈkʊdʒu/

1 <u>Could you</u> please open the window?
2 <u>Could you</u> please close the door?

6 **VOCABULARY / PRONUNCIATION PRACTICE** Look again at the Vocabulary. With a partner, take turns reading the requests aloud. Pay attention to blending of sounds in <u>Could you</u>.

NOW YOU CAN Ask for and agree to do a favor

1 ▶5:13 **CONVERSATION MODEL** Read and listen.

A: Could you do me a favor?
B: Of course.
A: It's very cold. Could you please close the window?
B: Sure. No problem.

▶5:15 **Ways to agree to a request**
Sure.
No problem.
Of course.
My pleasure.
OK.

2 ▶5:14 **RHYTHM AND INTONATION** Listen again and repeat. Then practice the Conversation Model with a partner.

3 **CONVERSATION ACTIVATOR** With a partner, change the conversation. Ask for a different favor. Then change roles.

A: Could you do me a favor?
B: ....
A: .... Could you please .... ?
B: ....

DON'T STOP!
Ask for more favors:
Could you please ___, too?

RECYCLE THIS LANGUAGE.
It's very [hot / windy].   I'm so [tired / hungry].
I'm making lunch.   I'm very busy right now.
I'm going to bed.

4 **CHANGE PARTNERS** Ask for other favors.

Ideas for favors
turn on the ___	help me
turn off the ___	do the laundry
open the ___	make dinner
close the ___	take out the garbage
hand me my ___	wash the dishes
	clean the house

UNIT 13 109

EXTENSION

1 ▶ 5:16 **READING** Read the article.

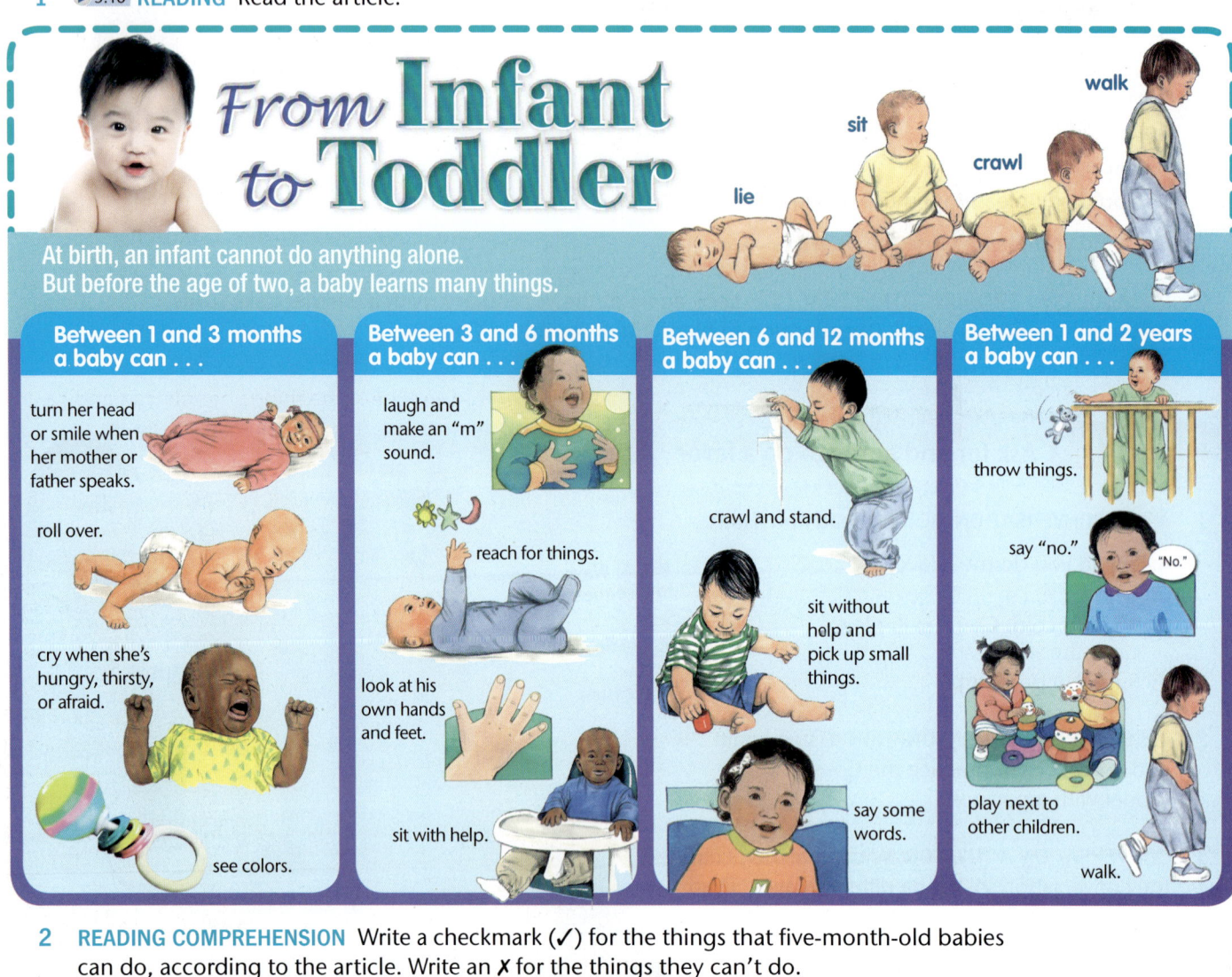

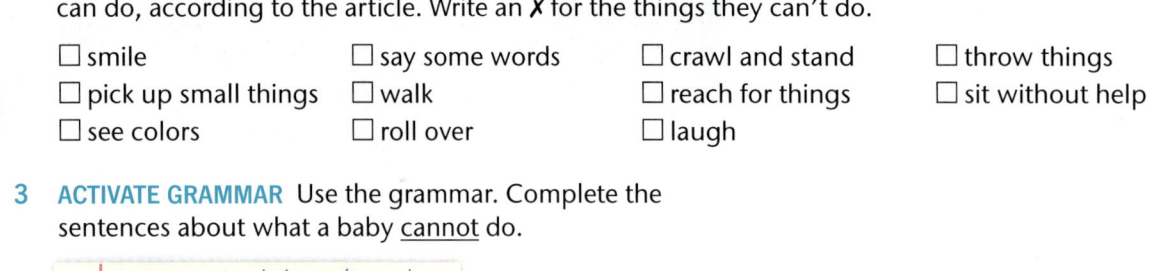

From Infant to Toddler

lie · sit · crawl · walk

At birth, an infant cannot do anything alone.
But before the age of two, a baby learns many things.

Between 1 and 3 months a baby can . . .
- turn her head or smile when her mother or father speaks.
- roll over.
- cry when she's hungry, thirsty, or afraid.
- see colors.

Between 3 and 6 months a baby can . . .
- laugh and make an "m" sound.
- reach for things.
- look at his own hands and feet.
- sit with help.

Between 6 and 12 months a baby can . . .
- crawl and stand.
- sit without help and pick up small things.
- say some words.

Between 1 and 2 years a baby can . . .
- throw things.
- say "no."
- play next to other children.
- walk.

2 **READING COMPREHENSION** Write a checkmark (✓) for the things that five-month-old babies can do, according to the article. Write an ✗ for the things they can't do.

- ☐ smile
- ☐ say some words
- ☐ crawl and stand
- ☐ throw things
- ☐ pick up small things
- ☐ walk
- ☐ reach for things
- ☐ sit without help
- ☐ see colors
- ☐ roll over
- ☐ laugh

3 **ACTIVATE GRAMMAR** Use the grammar. Complete the sentences about what a baby <u>cannot</u> do.

At one month, *a baby can't crawl.*
1 At two months,
2 At five months,
3 At eleven months,
4 At sixteen months,

4 **GROUP WORK** Discuss things children can and can't do at other ages.

"At three, a child can't ride a bicycle. But at eight, a child can do some household chores."

GRAMMAR BOOSTER
Unit 13 review • p. 144

For additional language practice . . .
♪ **TOP NOTCH POP** • Lyrics p. 150
"She Can't Play Guitar"
DIGITAL SONG · DIGITAL KARAOKE

REVIEW

PAIR WORK

1 Create conversations for the people.
   A: Let's ___.   B: I'm really sorry, but…

2 Ask and answer questions with <u>Can</u> about the people in Apartments 2A and 2B. For example:
   Can she ___? / Can he ___?

GAME Make true and false statements about the picture. For example:
   A: The girl in Apartment 2A is opening the window.
   B: That's false. She's closing the window.

STORY Create a story about what is happening in the apartment building. Start like this:
   It's 9:30. In Apartment 2B, a boy is playing the violin…

WRITING Describe some things people can and can't do when they are 80 years old. For example:

   At eighty, some people can't drive, but my grandfather can.

WRITING BOOSTER p. 149
Guidance for this writing exercise

Apartment 3A

Could you please ___?

Apartment 2A

Apartment 2B

Could you please ___?

NOW I CAN

☐ Discuss my abilities.
☐ Politely decline an invitation.
☐ Ask for and agree to do a favor.

Apartment 1A

UNIT 13

UNIT 14 Life Events and Plans

COMMUNICATION GOALS
1 Get to know someone's life story.
2 Discuss plans.
3 Share your dreams for the future.

LESSON 1 — GOAL: Get to know someone's life story

1 ▶5:19 **VOCABULARY** • *Some life events* Read and listen. Then listen again and repeat.

1 be born
2 grow up 
3 go to school 
4 move 
5 study 
6 graduate 

2 ▶5:20 **PRONUNCIATION** • *Diphthongs* Listen and repeat.

1 /aɪ/	2 /aʊ/	3 /ɔɪ/
my	how	boy
I	noun	oil
tie	town	boil

3 **PRONUNCIATION PRACTICE** Look at the Vocabulary pictures. Ask and answer the questions out loud with a partner. Use the correct pronunciation of the diphthongs.

1 What's the boy's first name?
2 What's his last name?
3 What school did he go to?
4 What university did he graduate from?

4 ▶5:21 **LISTENING COMPREHENSION** Listen to the conversation about Graciela Boyd's life story. Which statement about Graciela's life is true?

☐ She was born in Boston and lives there now.
☐ She was born in London and lives in Boston now.
☐ She was born in Costa Rica and lives in Boston now.

5 ▶5:22 Listen again. Circle the correct word or words to complete each statement. If necessary, listen again.

1 Graciela's mother is from (Costa Rica / Boston).
2 Graciela was born in (Costa Rica / London).
3 Her father is (American / British).
4 Graciela's mother is a/an (Spanish / English) teacher.
5 Graciela grew up in (London / Boston).
6 In May, Graciela is graduating from (the university / medical school).

6 **PAIR WORK** Use the questions to interview your partner. Then tell the class about your partner.

1 When and where were you born? What about other people in your family?
2 Where did you grow up? What about other people in your family?

112 UNIT 14

7 ▶5:23 **VOCABULARY** • *Academic subjects* Read and listen. Then listen again and repeat.

VOCABULARY BOOSTER
More academic subjects • p. 134

1 law
2 medicine 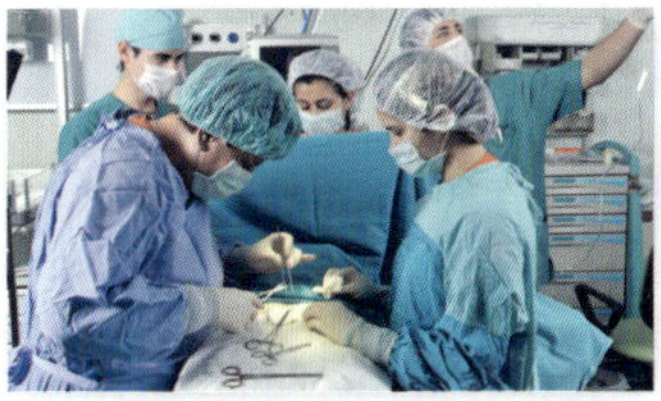
3 psychology 
4 business 
5 education 
6 engineering 
7 mathematics / math 
8 information technology 
9 nursing 
10 architecture 

NOW YOU CAN Get to know someone's life story

1 ▶5:24 **CONVERSATION MODEL** Read and listen.

A: Where were you born?
B: Here. In Houston.
A: And did you grow up here?
B: Yes, I did. And you?
A: I was born in Lima.
B: Did you grow up there?
A: Actually, no. I grew up in New York.

2 ▶5:25 **RHYTHM AND INTONATION** Listen again and repeat. Then practice the Conversation Model with a partner.

3 **CONVERSATION ACTIVATOR** With a partner, personalize the conversation with real information.

A: Where were you born?
B: ....
A: And did you grow up .... ?
B: .... And you?
A: I was born in ....
B: Did you grow up .... ?
A: ....

DON'T STOP!
Ask and answer more questions.

RECYCLE THIS LANGUAGE.
What do you do?
What are you studying?
 [or What did you study?]
Did you graduate?
How often did you move?

4 **CHANGE PARTNERS** Get to know another classmate's life story.

UNIT 14 113

LESSON 2 — GOAL: Discuss plans

1 ▶ 5:26 **VOCABULARY** • *More leisure activities* Read and listen. Then listen again and repeat.

VOCABULARY BOOSTER
More leisure activities • p. 134

1 travel
2 go camping 
3 go fishing 
4 relax 
5 hang out with friends 
6 sleep late 
7 do nothing 

Also remember:
check e-mail
exercise
go dancing
go out for dinner
go running
go to the beach
go to the movies
listen to music
paint
play soccer
read
take a nap
visit friends

2 ▶ 5:27 **LISTENING COMPREHENSION** Listen to the phone calls. Complete each sentence with the present continuous form of one of the words or phrases from the Vocabulary.

1 Charlie is *doing nothing* ....
2 Rachel's ....
3 They're .... on Saturday.
4 Barbara's ....
5 Harvey's family is ....

3 **GRAMMAR** • *Be going to* + base form

Use **be going to** + base form to express future plans.

I'm
You're
He's
She's   **going to relax** this weekend.
We're
They're

I'm
You're
He's
She's   **not going to go** camping this weekend.
We're
They're

Contractions
is not going / 's not going / isn't going
are not going / 're not going / aren't going

Yes / no questions
Are you **going to sleep** late tomorrow?   Yes, I am. / No, I'm not.
Is she **going to travel** to Europe?   Yes, she is. / No, she isn't.
Are we **going to be** on time?   Yes, we are. / No, we aren't.

114   UNIT 14

4 GRAMMAR PRACTICE Write sentences about future plans with be going to.

1 you / eat in a restaurant / this weekend? *Are you going to eat in a restaurant this weekend?*
2 They / go to the movies / tonight. ....
3 I / hang out with my parents / at the beach. ....
4 he / relax / tomorrow? ....
5 she / go fishing / with you? ....
6 we / exercise / on Saturday? ....
7 they / move? ....
8 Jeff and Joan / study / architecture. ....
9 She / graduate / in May. ....

NOW YOU CAN Discuss plans

1 ▶5:28 **CONVERSATION MODEL** Read and listen.

A: Any plans for the weekend?
B: Not really. I'm just going to hang out with friends. And you?
A: Actually, I'm going to go camping.

2 ▶5:29 **RHYTHM AND INTONATION** Listen again and repeat. Then practice the Conversation Model with a partner.

3 **CONVERSATION ACTIVATOR** With a partner, personalize the conversation. Use the Vocabulary or the pictures below and be going to.

A: Any plans for .... ?
B: .... I'm .... And you?
A: Actually, I'm ....

DON'T STOP!
Ask about other times. Ask more questions with be going to.

RECYCLE THIS LANGUAGE.
Are you going to ___ [tonight / tomorrow / next week / after class]? How about [next weekend / the day after tomorrow]?

4 **CHANGE PARTNERS** Ask another classmate about his or her plans.

UNIT 14 115

LESSON 3

GOAL Share your dreams for the future

1 ▶ 5:30 **VOCABULARY** • *Some dreams for the future* Read and listen. Then listen again and repeat.

1 I'd like to **get married**.
2 I'd like to **have children**. 
3 I'd like to **retire**. 
4 I'd like to **change careers**. 
5 I'd like to **travel**. 
6 I'd like to **make a lot of money**. 
7 I'd like to **give money to charity**. 
8 I'd like to **live a long life**. 

2 ▶ 5:31 **LISTENING COMPREHENSION** Listen and complete each sentence with the Vocabulary.

1 She'd like to ...*get married*... .
2 He'd like to ....
3 She'd like to ....
4 He'd like to ....
5 She'd like to ....
6 She'd like to ....
7 He'd like to ....
8 She'd like to ....

3 **ACTIVATE VOCABULARY** Complete the survey by checking the boxes for your dreams for the future.

In the next two years, I'd like to...

- ☐ get married
- ☐ graduate
- ☐ travel
- ☐ have children
- ☐ move to a new country
- ☐ move to a new city
- ☐ move to a new apartment or a new house
- ☐ study a new language
- ☐ write a book
- ☐ make a lot of money
- ☐ give money to charity
- ☐ learn to play a musical instrument
- ☐ get a new car
- ☐ meet a good-looking man
- ☐ meet a good-looking woman
- ☐ change careers
- ☐ retire
- ☐ paint my living room
- ☐ buy a new refrigerator
- ☐ OTHER *I'd like to...*

4 **VOCABULARY PRACTICE** On the notepad, write three of your dreams from the survey on page 116.

> *I'd like to move to a new city.*

5 **PAIR WORK** Compare surveys with a partner. Ask and answer questions.

" I'd like to write a book. What about you? "

" Me? I'd like to change careers! "

NOW YOU CAN Share your dreams for the future

1 ▶ 5:32 **CONVERSATION MODEL** Read and listen.

A: So what are your dreams for the future?
B: Well, I'd like to get married and have children. What about you?
A: Me? Actually, I'd like to study art.
B: Really? That's great.

2 ▶ 5:33 **RHYTHM AND INTONATION** Listen again and repeat. Then practice the Conversation Model with a partner.

3 **CONVERSATION ACTIVATOR** With a partner, personalize the conversation. Use the Vocabulary from page 116 and real information.

A: So what are your dreams for the future?
B: Well, I'd like to ………. What about you?
A: Me? Actually, I'd like to ……….
B: Really? That's great.

DON'T STOP!
Talk about other plans.

RECYCLE THIS LANGUAGE.
Really?
No kidding!
Sounds nice. / Sounds good.

4 **CHANGE PARTNERS** Ask another classmate what he or she would like to do.

UNIT 14 117

EXTENSION

1 ▶ 5:34 **READING** Read about Harry Houdini, a famous escape artist.

The Amazing HOUDINI

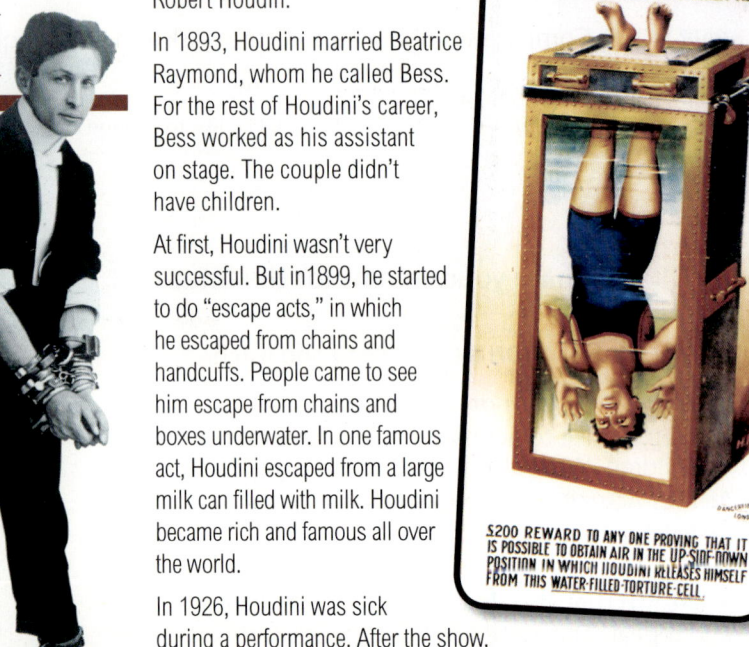

Harry Houdini was born Ehrich Weisz in Budapest, Hungary, on March 24, 1874. He came from a large family. He had six siblings—five brothers and one sister.

At the age of four, Ehrich moved with his family to the United States, first to Appleton, Wisconsin, and then later to New York City.

The family was poor, and young Ehrich didn't get an education and never graduated from school. Instead, he worked to help the family. Ehrich and his brother Theo were interested in magic, and at the age of seventeen, Ehrich began his career as a magician. He changed his name to Houdini, after the name of a famous French magician, Robert Houdin.

In 1893, Houdini married Beatrice Raymond, whom he called Bess. For the rest of Houdini's career, Bess worked as his assistant on stage. The couple didn't have children.

At first, Houdini wasn't very successful. But in 1899, he started to do "escape acts," in which he escaped from chains and handcuffs. People came to see him escape from chains and boxes underwater. In one famous act, Houdini escaped from a large milk can filled with milk. Houdini became rich and famous all over the world.

In 1926, Houdini was sick during a performance. After the show, he went to the hospital. But it was too late—Harry Houdini died at the young age of 52.

2 **READING COMPREHENSION** Answer the questions in complete sentences.

1. What was Houdini's original name? ....
2. Where was he born? ....
3. When did his family move? ....
4. Where did they move? ....
5. Did Houdini graduate from a university? ....
6. Did Houdini get married? ....
7. What was his wife's name? ....
8. Did the Houdinis have children? ....
9. When did Houdini die? ....
10. **Challenge:** Do you want to know more about Houdini? Write three information questions about Houdini. Example:

    Why did Houdini's family move to the United States?

3 **PAIR WORK** Tell your partner your life story. Ask your partner questions about his or her story.

GRAMMAR BOOSTER
Unit 14 review • p. 145

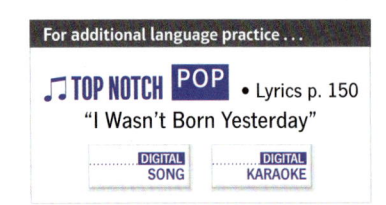

For additional language practice...
♪ **TOP NOTCH POP** • Lyrics p. 150
"I Wasn't Born Yesterday"

REVIEW

PAIR WORK Ask and answer questions about Miranda Lewis's life. Ask about her plans and her dreams for the future. For example:
Where was Miranda born?

TELL A STORY Tell the story of Miranda's life. Talk about the past, the present, and the future. What did she do? What is she doing now? What would she like to do? Start like this:
Miranda was born in 1993. She grew up in …

WRITING Write the story of your own life and about your plans and dreams for the future. Include a picture or pictures if possible. For example:
I was born in Madrid in 1986. I grew up in …

WRITING BOOSTER p. 149
Guidance for this writing exercise

Miranda Lewis
Born August 3, 1993
San Antonio (U.S.)

1995–2008
Miranda's house
Atlanta (U.S.)

May 12, 2013
Millerton State Business College
Las Vegas (U.S.)

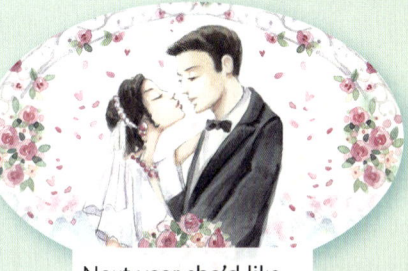

Next year she'd like…

In three years she'd like…

Miranda today
Los Angeles (U.S.)

✓ NOW I CAN

- ☐ Get to know someone's life story.
- ☐ Discuss plans.
- ☐ Share my dreams for the future.

Units 8–14 REVIEW

1 ▶ 5:37 **LISTENING COMPREHENSION** Listen to the conversations. Check the picture that answers each question.

1 Where does he live?
a ☐ b ☐

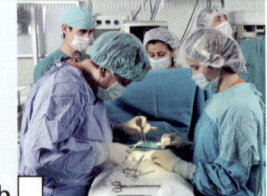

2 Where does he work?
a ☐ b ☐

3 Where does she work?
a ☐ b ☐

4 Where does she teach?
a ☐ b ☐

5 Where does she work?
a ☐ b ☐

6 Where does his daughter work?
a ☐ b ☐

2 **VOCABULARY / GRAMMAR PRACTICE** Complete the e-mail about Anna's new apartment. Use <u>there's</u> and <u>there are</u> and the names of furniture and appliances.

My new apartment!

Hey, Mel: I have this great furnished apartment. It has everything! The ....1............ has a nice big stove and four ....2............ . There's a dining room with a ....3............ and four ....4............ . Next to the dining room ....5............ a large living room with a green ....6............ . And ....7............ four chairs: great for hanging out with my friends and watching ....8............ . There's no office, but there's a ....9............ in the living room. And I love the bedroom. It has a ....10............ for all my books. There are two ....11............ and two blue ....12............ . Very nice! There's even a beautiful balcony next to the bedroom, with a little ....13............ and two ....14............ . The bathroom is the only room that isn't perfect. ....15............ a shower but no ....16............ .

120 UNITS 8–14 REVIEW

3 GRAMMAR PRACTICE Write questions about home and work. Use <u>What</u>, <u>Where</u>, <u>Is there</u>, and <u>Are there</u>. Answer the questions with true information.

Your questions	Your answers
1 Is there a closet in your bedroom?	1 Yes, there is.
2	2
3	3
4	4
5	5
6	6

4 GRAMMAR PRACTICE Complete the conversations with the correct forms of the verbs.

1 **A:** Where .... Jill .... last weekend?
      _{go}
   B: I'm not sure. I know she .... to go camping.
      _{want}
   A: Maybe she .... camping, then.
      _{go}

2 **A:** Are you going to go to the beach today?
   B: No way. We .... there yesterday.
      _{be}
   We .... an awful time.
      _{have}
   A: Why? What .... wrong?
      _{be}
   B: The water .... really dirty, so I
      _{be}
   .... swimming.
      _{not go}

3 **A:** Where .... you this morning?
      _{be}
   B: Me? I .... running.
      _{go}
   A: Did Sheri .... with you?
      _{go}
   B: No. She .... to class.
      _{go}

4 **A:** .... you .... yesterday?
              _{work}
   B: No, I .... Yesterday I .... sick.
                                                _{be}
   A: I'm sorry. .... you .... a fever?
                                        _{have}
   B: Yes, I ....

5 CONVERSATION PRACTICE Use the questions you wrote in Grammar Practice 3. Exchange real information about where you live and work. Start like this:

" What's your apartment like? "

Ideas
- the location of your home, school, and workplace
- the places in your neighborhood
- the description of your home

UNITS 8–14 REVIEW 121

6 GRAMMAR PRACTICE
Complete the telephone conversations with the present continuous or the simple present tense.

1 A: Hello?

B: Hi, Sid. Ann. .... ?
   you / sleep

A: No, I'm not. .... breakfast.
   I / make

B: .... breakfast?
   you / usually / make

A: Actually, ... often.
   I / not cook
   But .... for a test.
   Gwen / study

2 A: Hello?

B: Hi, Bonnie. .... for food.
   I / shop
   .... anything from the store?
   you / need

A: Actually, yes. .... a salad for
   I / make
   dinner and .... any tomatoes.
   I / not have

B: No problem. .... those
   They / sell
   beautiful tomatoes from Mexico right now.

A: Great! .... those tomatoes.
   I / like

3 A: Hello?

B: Hi, Liz. Where are you?

A: .... right now. Can I
   I / drive
   call you back?

B: Sure. .... my office
   you have
   number? .... today.
   I / work

4 A: Hello?

B: Hi, Stan. What time ....
   you / get up
   on Saturdays?

A: Why .... that now?
   you / ask
   It's only Thursday!

B: Because .... her driving
   Maria / take
   test at 8:30, and .... a ride to
   she / need
   the test.

7 PAIR WORK
Partner A: Look at your picture. Partner B: Turn your book and look at your picture. Ask questions about the foods on the table.

" Are there any apples on your table? "

" No, there aren't. "

PARTNER A

PARTNER B

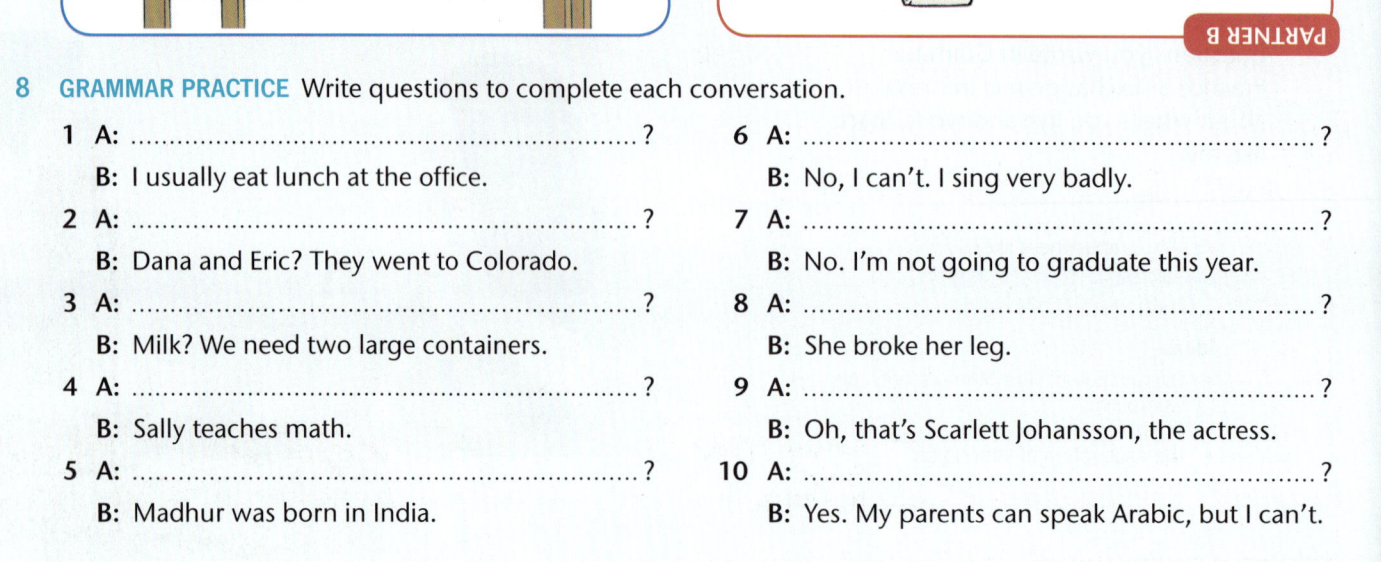

8 GRAMMAR PRACTICE
Write questions to complete each conversation.

1 A: .... ?
B: I usually eat lunch at the office.

2 A: .... ?
B: Dana and Eric? They went to Colorado.

3 A: .... ?
B: Milk? We need two large containers.

4 A: .... ?
B: Sally teaches math.

5 A: .... ?
B: Madhur was born in India.

6 A: .... ?
B: No, I can't. I sing very badly.

7 A: .... ?
B: No. I'm not going to graduate this year.

8 A: .... ?
B: She broke her leg.

9 A: .... ?
B: Oh, that's Scarlett Johansson, the actress.

10 A: .... ?
B: Yes. My parents can speak Arabic, but I can't.

9 ▶5:38 **LISTENING COMPREHENSION** Listen to the conversations. Check Past, Present, or Future. Then listen again and check your work.

	Past	Present	Future
1	☐	✓	☐
2	☐	☐	☐
3	☐	☐	☐
4	☐	☐	☐
5	☐	☐	☐
6	☐	☐	☐

10 **VOCABULARY / GRAMMAR PRACTICE** Express sympathy to each person. Make suggestions with should and shouldn't.

1 I have a terrible headache.
YOU *I'm so sorry*. You *should take something*.

2 My husband is making lunch and he burned his hand!
YOU .... He ....

3 My brother and I have stomachaches. I think we ate something bad.
YOU .... You ....

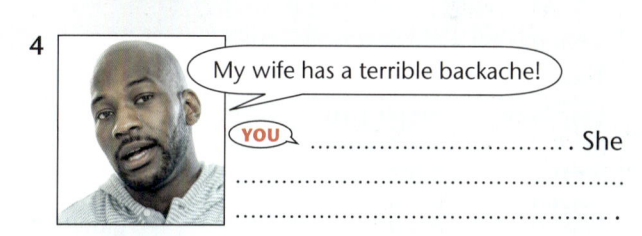

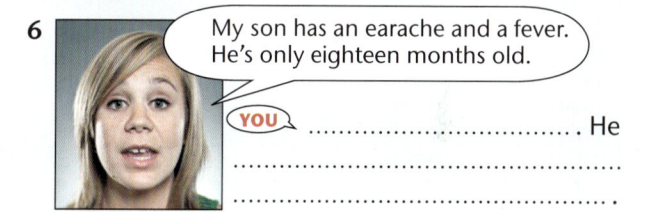

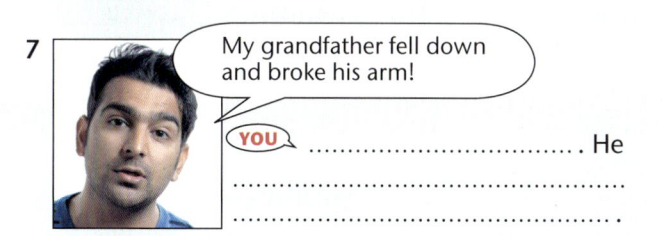

4 My wife has a terrible backache!
YOU .... She ....

5 I didn't sleep last night. I feel terrible!
YOU .... You ....

6 My son has an earache and a fever. He's only eighteen months old.
YOU .... He ....

7 My grandfather fell down and broke his arm!
YOU .... He ....

11 **CONVERSATION PRACTICE** Discuss relatives and friends. Start like this:

Ideas
- Appearance
- Studies
- Abilities
- Life events
- Dreams for the future

❝ Tell me about your mother. Where was she born? ❞

RECYCLE THIS LANGUAGE.
And your [father]?
Really?
No kidding.

Reference Charts

COUNTRIES AND NATIONALITIES

Country	Nationality	Country	Nationality	Country	Nationality
Argentina	Argentinean / Argentine	Guatemala	Guatemalan	Peru	Peruvian
Australia	Australian	Holland	Dutch	Poland	Polish
Belgium	Belgian	Honduras	Honduran	Portugal	Portuguese
Bolivia	Bolivian	Hungary	Hungarian	Russia	Russian
Brazil	Brazilian	India	Indian	Saudi Arabia	Saudi / Saudi Arabian
Canada	Canadian	Indonesia	Indonesian	Spain	Spanish
Chile	Chilean	Ireland	Irish	Sweden	Swedish
China	Chinese	Italy	Italian	Switzerland	Swiss
Colombia	Colombian	Japan	Japanese	Taiwan	Chinese
Costa Rica	Costa Rican	Korea	Korean	Thailand	Thai
Ecuador	Ecuadorian	Lebanon	Lebanese	Turkey	Turkish
Egypt	Egyptian	Malaysia	Malaysian	the United Kingdom	British
El Salvador	Salvadorean	Mexico	Mexican	the United States	American
France	French	Nicaragua	Nicaraguan	Uruguay	Uruguayan
Germany	German	Panama	Panamanian	Venezuela	Venezuelan
Greece	Greek	Paraguay	Paraguayan	Vietnam	Vietnamese

NUMBERS 100 TO 1,000,000,000

100	one hundred	1,000	one thousand	10,000	ten thousand	1,000,000	one million
500	five hundred	5,000	five thousand	100,000	one hundred thousand	1,000,000,000	one billion

IRREGULAR VERBS

This is an alphabetical list of all irregular verbs in the *Top Notch Fundamentals* units.

base form	simple past	base form	simple past	base form	simple past
be	was / were	get	got	say	said
break	broke	give	gave	see	saw
bring	brought	go	went	sing	sang
buy	bought	grow	grew	sit	sat
choose	chose	hang out	hung out	sleep	slept
come	came	have	had	stand	stood
cut	cut	hear	heard	swim	swam
do	did	hurt	hurt	take	took
draw	drew	lie	lay	teach	taught
drink	drank	make	made	tell	told
drive	drove	meet	met	think	thought
eat	ate	put	put	throw	threw
fall	fell	read	read	wear	wore
feel	felt	ride	rode	write	wrote
find	found				

PRONUNCIATION TABLE

These are the pronunciation symbols used in *Top Notch Fundamentals*.

Vowels

Symbol	Key Words	Symbol	Key Words
i	feed	ə	banana, around
ɪ	did	ɚ	shirt, birthday
eɪ	date, table	aɪ	cry, eye
ɛ	bed, neck	aʊ	about, how
æ	bad, hand	ɔɪ	boy
ɑ	box, father	ɪr	here, near
ɔ	wash	ɛr	chair
oʊ	comb, post	ɑr	guitar, are
ʊ	book, good	ɔr	door, chore
u	boot, food, student	ʊr	tour
ʌ	but, mother		

Consonants

Symbol	Key Words	Symbol	Key Words
p	park, happy	t	butter, bottle
b	back, cabbage	t̚	button
t	tie	ʃ	she, station, special, discussion
d	die	ʒ	leisure
k	came, kitchen, quarter	h	hot, who
g	game, go	m	men
tʃ	chicken, watch	n	sun, know
dʒ	jacket, orange	ŋ	sung, singer
f	face, photographer	w	week, white
v	vacation	l	light, long
θ	thing, math	r	rain, writer
ð	then, that	y	yes, use, music
s	city, psychology		
z	please, goes		

Vocabulary Booster

UNIT 8

▶ 5:47 **MORE HOME AND OFFICE VOCABULARY**

1. a roof
2. a fence
3. a driveway
4. an intercom 
5. a doorbell 
6. a fire escape 
7. a pillow 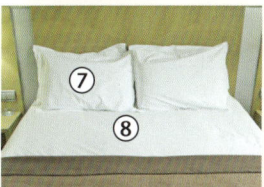 
8. a sheet
9. a blanket
10. a shower curtain  
11. a bath mat
12. a faucet 
13. towels 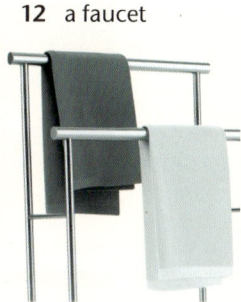
14. a medicine cabinet 
15. toothpaste 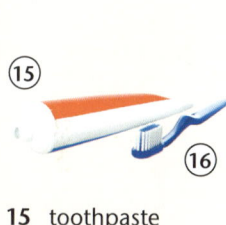
16. a toothbrush
17. a burner 
18. an oven
19. a dishwasher 
20. a coffee maker 
21. a ladle 
22. a pot
23. a food processor 
24. a napkin 
25. a place mat
26. a glass
27. a fork 
28. a knife
29. a tablespoon / a soup spoon
30. a teaspoon
31. a plate 
32. a bowl
33. a cup
34. a saucer
35. a filing cabinet 
36. a fax machine 

Write five statements. Use the Vocabulary.
For example:
My apartment has a fire escape.
I have blue plates and bowls in my cabinets.

UNIT 9

▶ 5:48 **MORE WEATHER VOCABULARY**

1 a thunderstorm

2 a snowstorm

3 a hurricane

4 a tornado

▶ 5:49 **THE FOUR SEASONS**

1 spring

2 summer

3 fall / autumn

4 winter

Write four statements about the weather and seasons pictures.
For example: *It's not raining.*

130 VOCABULARY BOOSTER

UNIT 10

▶ 5:50 **MORE VEGETABLES**

1 carrots
2 brussels sprouts
3 leeks
4 cabbage
5 broccoli
6 cauliflower
7 lettuce
8 corn
9 peas
10 asparagus
11 cucumbers
12 an eggplant
13 beans
14 celery
15 garlic

▶ 5:51 **MORE FRUITS**

1 a grapefruit
2 a lime
3 a pineapple
4 grapes
5 a pear
6 an apricot
7 a peach
8 a strawberry
9 a raspberry
10 an avocado
11 a papaya
12 a mango
13 a kiwi
14 a watermelon
15 raisins
16 figs
17 prunes
18 dates

Write five statements about the fruits and vegetables you and your family like.
For example: *I like avocadoes. My sister doesn't like avocadoes.*

VOCABULARY BOOSTER

UNIT 11

▶ 5:52 **MORE OUTDOOR ACTIVITIES**

1 go horseback riding
2 go sailing 
3 play golf 
4 go rollerblading 
5 go snorkeling 
6 go rock climbing 
7 go ice skating 
8 go windsurfing 

> Write five sentences to describe the photos. Use the simple past tense.
> For example: *She went horseback riding.*

UNIT 12

▶ 5:53 **MORE PARTS OF THE BODY**

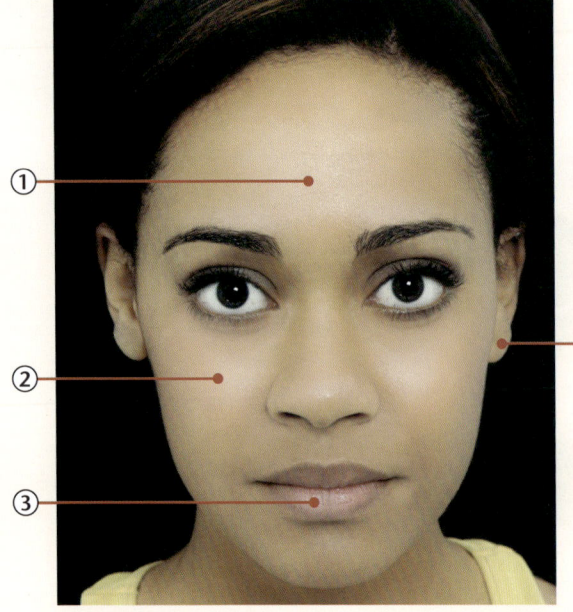

1 forehead
2 cheek
3 lip
4 earlobe
5 tongue
6 elbow
7 thigh
8 calf

> Describe one of the people. Write three statements. Use the Vocabulary from Unit 12.
> For example: *She has straight brown hair.*

132 VOCABULARY BOOSTER

UNIT 13

▶ 5:54 **MORE MUSICAL INSTRUMENTS**

1. a cello
2. a piano
3. a tuba
4. a trumpet
5. a trombone
6. a flute
7. a clarinet
8. a saxophone
9. a xylophone
10. a recorder
11. an accordion
12. drums

> **Write four statements with the Vocabulary. Use can / can't and the adverbs well and badly.**
> For example:
>   *My sister can play the piano well.*
>   *My father plays the accordion badly.*

VOCABULARY BOOSTER

UNIT 14

▶ 5:55 MORE ACADEMIC SUBJECTS

1 art
2 drama 
3 science 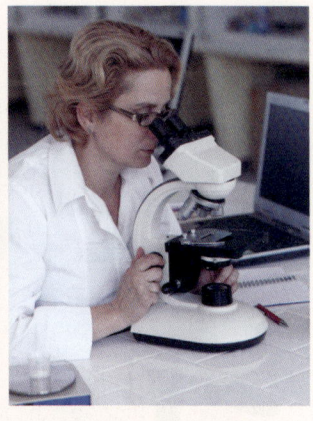
4 biology 
5 chemistry 
6 history 

▶ 5:56 MORE LEISURE ACTIVITIES

1 go skiing
2 go hiking 
3 play 
4 garden 
5 go on a cruise 
6 get a manicure 

Write four statements, using **I'd like to** or **be going to** and the Unit 14 Vocabulary. Include time expressions.

For example:

I'd like to study fine art in the future.
I'm not going to go on a cruise this year.

134 VOCABULARY BOOSTER

Grammar Booster

The Grammar Booster is optional. It contains extra practice of each unit's grammar.

UNIT 8

1. Write questions with Where. Use a question mark (?).
   1. your grandparents / live *Where do your grandparents live?*
   2. John's friend / go shopping ……………………………………………
   3. her brother / study English ……………………………………………
   4. you / eat breakfast ……………………………………………
   5. they / listen to music ……………………………………………
   6. Rob and Nancy / exercise ……………………………………………
   7. his mother / work ……………………………………………
   8. your brother / do the laundry ……………………………………………

2. Complete the statements with in, on, at, or to.
   1. His house is ..*on*.......... Barker Street.
   2. They work ……………… the tenth floor.
   3. Ms. Cruz takes the train ……………… work.
   4. It's ……………… 18 Spencer Street.
   5. Jack studies French ……………… the BTI Institute.
   6. Mr. Klein works ……………… the hospital.
   7. Ms. Anderson's office is ……………… the fifth floor.
   8. Jason's sister works ……………… 5 Main Street.

3. Complete each sentence with There's or There are.
   1. ...*There's*.... a movie at noon.
   2. ……………… a concert at 2:00 and a game at 3:00.
   3. ……………… a bank on the corner of Main and 12th Street.
   4. ……………… two apartment buildings across the street.
   5. ……………… bookstores nearby.
   6. ……………… a pharmacy and a newsstand around the corner.
   7. ……………… two dressers in the bedroom.
   8. ……………… three elevators in the Smith Building.

4. Write questions with Is there or Are there. Use a question mark (?).
   1. a dance / this weekend *Is there a dance this weekend?*
   2. three meetings / this week ……………………………………………
   3. a bank / nearby ……………………………………………
   4. how many / games / this afternoon ……………………………………………
   5. how many / pharmacies / on 3rd Avenue ……………………………………………
   6. how many / parties / this month ……………………………………………

UNIT 9

1 Write the present participle of the following base forms.

1. rain *raining*
2. snow ....
3. watch ....
4. eat ....
5. take ....
6. drive ....
7. check ....
8. make ....
9. do ....
10. exercise ....
11. shave ....
12. put ....
13. comb ....
14. brush ....
15. come ....
16. wear ....
17. shop ....
18. go ....
19. study ....
20. listen ....
21. wash ....
22. play ....
23. read ....
24. clean ....
25. work ....
26. write ....
27. talk ....
28. buy ....

2 Check (✓) the sentences that indicate a future plan.

- [✓] 1 On Tuesday I'm working at home.
- [ ] 2 I'm watching TV right now.
- [ ] 3 Is Marina taking a shower?
- [ ] 4 Where is she going tomorrow night?
- [ ] 5 Jen's eating dinner.
- [ ] 6 I'm driving to the mall this afternoon.
- [ ] 7 I'm studying Arabic this year. My teacher is very good.
- [ ] 8 Who's making dinner on Saturday?

3 Complete each conversation with the present continuous.

1. A: *What are you doing* ?

      what / you / do

   B: .... my hair.

     I / wash

2. A: .... ?

   where / she / drive

   B: .... to the bookstore.

   she / go

3. A: .... the bus?

   why / he / take

   B: Because ....

               it / rain

4. A: .... at home tonight?

   we / eat

   B: No. .... out for dinner.

      we / go

5. A: .... a dress to the party?

   Maya / wear

   B: No. .... a dress. .... pants.

       she / not wear   she / wear

UNIT 10

1 Complete each question with How much or How many.

1. *How much* sugar do you want in your coffee?
2. .... onions do you need for the potato pancakes?
3. .... cans of coffee are there on the shelf?
4. .... meat do you eat every day?
5. .... loaves of bread do we need for dinner?
6. .... pepper would you like in your chicken salad?
7. .... bottles of oil does she need from the store?
8. .... eggs do you eat every week?
9. .... oranges are there? I want to make orange juice.
10. .... pasta would you like?

2 Choose the correct word or phrase to complete each statement. Circle the letter.

1. I .... English every day.
   a am studying   **(b) study**
2. We usually .... the bus to work.
   a are taking   b take
3. Annemarie .... the kitchen now.
   a is cleaning   b cleans
4. He really .... lemonade.
   a is liking   b likes
5. This store .... beautiful clothes.
   a is having   b has
6. On Wednesdays I .... dinner for my parents.
   a am cooking   b cook
7. They never .... coffee.
   a are drinking   b drink
8. Our children .... TV on weekdays.
   a are watching   b don't watch

UNIT 11

1 Complete the conversations with the past tense of be.

1. A: Where *were* Paul and Jackie last night?
   B: I don't know, but they .... here.
2. A: .... she at school yesterday?
   B: No. She .... at home.
3. A: When .... you in Italy? Last year?
   B: Last year? No, we .... in Italy last year.
   We .... there in 2012.
4. A: What time .... the movie?
   B: It .... at 7:00.
5. A: .... your parents at home at 10:00 last night?
   B: No. They .... at a play.
6. A: Who .... at work on Monday?
   B: Barry and Anne .... But I ....

2 First complete each question. Use the simple past tense. Then write a true answer. Begin each answer with a capital letter. End with a period (.).

1 ...*Did*... you ..*go*.......... to work yesterday?
   go
   YOU ....

2 What time .... you .... dinner?
   make
   YOU ....

3 What .... you .... for breakfast?
   eat
   YOU ....

4 Who .... breakfast with you?
   eat
   YOU ....

5 What .... you .... this week?
   buy
   YOU ....

UNIT 12

1 Write (a) a sentence with <u>be</u> and (b) a sentence with <u>have</u>. Use a period (.)

1 Kate / hair / long / straight
   a *Kate's hair is long and straight.*
   b *Kate has long straight hair.*

2 George / short / black / hair
   a ....
   b ....

3 Harry / long / curly / hair
   a ....
   b ....

4 Mary / eyes / blue
   a ....
   b ....

5 Adam / beard / gray
   a ....
   b ....

6 Amy / pretty / eyes
   a ....
   b ....

2 Complete each sentence with <u>should</u> and a verb from the box.

1 It's your birthday. You ..*should go*.............. out for dinner!
2 I'm sorry you have a toothache. You .... a dentist.
3 There's a movie on TV tonight. We .... it.
4 You have a cold? You .... today.
5 We have tomatoes, potatoes, and onions. We .... tomato potato soup for dinner tonight!
6 Pam's taking a shower right now. You .... back later.
7 Martin has a headache. He .... soccer tonight.
8 It's time for bed. You .... undressed.

call
(not) exercise
go
watch
make
(not) play
see
get

UNIT 13

1 Write sentences with the simple present tense and the adverbs <u>well</u> or <u>badly</u>. Begin each sentence with a capital letter. End with a period (.).

1. my father / sing / really well ..My father sings really well.............
2. my mother / cook French food / well ....
3. my grandfather / play the guitar / badly ....
4. my grandmother / sew clothes / very well
   ....
5. my sister / knit sweaters / well ....
6. my friend / draw pictures / really well ....
7. I / play the violin / badly ....

2 Answer each question with true information. Use short answers with <u>can</u> or <u>can't</u>. Begin each answer with a capital letter. End with a period (.)

1. Can you play the piano? ....
2. Can you ski? ....
3. Can your parents sing well? ....
4. Can your friends speak English? ....
5. Can you draw? ....
6. Can your father fix things? ....

3 Complete each sentence. Use <u>too</u> and an adjective.

1. I need a new dress. This dress is ..too old.............. .

2. This skirt is .... I want a short skirt.

GRAMMAR BOOSTER 144

3 His shirt is .... He needs size small.

4 I don't want that suit. It's ....

5 He needs size medium. This shirt is ....

UNIT 14

1 Answer the following questions with true information. Use <u>be going to</u>. Begin each answer with a capital letter. End with a period (.).

1 Are your classmates going to study tonight? ....
2 Are you going to relax this weekend? ....
3 Are you going to exercise today? ....
4 Are you going to make dinner tonight? ....
5 Are you going to move in the next two years? ....
6 Are you going to check your e-mail today? ....
7 Are you going to hang out with your friends or family this weekend? ....

2 Write a question with <u>be going to</u> for each answer. Don't use the verb <u>do</u>. Begin each question with a capital letter. End with a question mark (?).

1 *Are you going to go to the movies tonight?* .... Yes. I'm going to go to the movies tonight.
2 .... Yes. They're going to eat in a restaurant after the concert.
3 .... Yes. Carla's brother is going to go fishing with her.
4 .... Yes. I'm going to go to work tomorrow.
5 .... No. He's not going to graduate this year.
6 .... Yes. They're going to take the bus to school.

Writing Booster

The Writing Booster is optional. It gives guidance for the writing task on the last page of each unit.

UNIT 8

Guided Writing Practice Choose one of the homes in the Reading on page 70. Write the features of that home and your home in the chart.

On a separate sheet of paper, compare the two homes in the chart. Use <u>and</u> and <u>but</u>.

Example:

> Eduardo's home is an apartment, and I live in an apartment, too. There's an elevator in his building, but we don't have an elevator. In his apartment, there are . . .

	his or her home	my home
Is it a house or apartment?		
How many bedrooms are there?		
How many bathrooms are there?		
Is the kitchen small or large?		
Is there an office?		
Is there a garage or an elevator?		
Is there a garden?		
Is there a view?		
Other features?		

UNIT 9

Guided Writing Practice Write answers to some or all of the following questions about your plans for the week. Use time expressions.

What are you doing right now?
What are you doing this evening?
What are you doing tomorrow?
Are you doing anything special this weekend?
What are you doing on Saturday and Sunday?

Example:

> Right now, I'm writing about my plans for the week. This evening, I'm checking e-mail and . . .

UNIT 10

Guided Writing Practice Answer some or all of the questions to help you write what you eat on a typical day. Use frequency adverbs <u>sometimes</u>, <u>usually</u>, and <u>always</u>. Use time expressions <u>every day</u>, <u>once a week</u>, <u>twice a week</u>, etc.

What do you eat for breakfast on weekdays?
What do you eat for breakfast on weekends?
What time do you usually eat your meals?
Do you eat after school or work?
How many times a week (or month) do you go out for dinner?

Example: On weekdays, I usually eat breakfast at 9:00. I always eat bread and eggs, and . . .

UNIT 11

Guided Writing Practice Write about your weekend. Use past time expressions. Answer some or all of the questions to guide your writing.

Did you have a good time last weekend?
How was the weather?
What did you do on Friday night?
What did you do on Saturday?
What did you do on Sunday?

Example: *Last weekend, I had a great time . . .*

UNIT 12

Guided Writing Practice Choose a person you want to describe. On a separate sheet of paper, answer the questions in your description.

Who is this person?
How old is the person?
Is he or she tall or short?
Is he or she good-looking?
What color is his or her hair?
Is it short or long? Straight, wavy, or curly?
What color are his or her eyes?
Does he or she wear glasses?

Example:
Mary Blake is my classmate, and she is twenty years old. She's very tall and pretty, and . . .

UNIT 13

Guided Writing Practice What can people do when they are eighty years old? Complete the chart. Then use the information from the chart to write about the topic. Write on a separate sheet of paper. Write as much as you can.

Example: *Old people can't do some things, but sometimes they can . . .*

	Yes, they can.	They can sometimes.	No, they can't.
work	☐	☐	☐
cook meals	☐	☐	☐
live on the second floor	☐	☐	☐
get dressed	☐	☐	☐
take a shower or bath	☐	☐	☐
clean the house	☐	☐	☐
exercise / go running / go bike riding	☐	☐	☐
drive a car	☐	☐	☐
go dancing	☐	☐	☐
other	☐	☐	☐

UNIT 14

Guided Writing Practice Write the story of your own life. Then write your plans and dreams for the future. Answer some or all of the following questions in your story. Write on a separate sheet of paper. Write as much as you can.

Where were you born?
Where do you live now?
Where did you grow up?
What school did you go to?
What did you study? (Or what are you studying now?)
Did you graduate?
What are your dreams for the future? (Write *I'd like . . .*)

Example: *I was born on September 3rd, 1999 in . . .*

Top Notch Pop Lyrics

▶ 1:30/1:31 **What Do You Do?** [Unit 1]

(CHORUS)
What do you do?
What do you do?
I'm a student.
You're a teacher.
She's a doctor.
He's a nurse.
What about you?
What do you do?
I'm a florist.
You're a gardener.
He's a waiter.
She's a chef.
Do-do-do-do…
That's what we do.
It's nice to meet you.
What's your name?
Can you spell that, please?
Thank you.
Yes, it's nice to meet you, too.

(CHORUS)
We are artists and musicians,
architects, and electricians.
How about you?
What do you do?
We are bankers,
we are dentists,
engineers, and flight attendants.
Do-do-do-do…
That's what we do.
Hi, I'm Linda. Are you John?
No, he's right over there.
Excuse me. Thank you very much.
Good-bye.
Do-do-do-do…
Do-do-do-do…
Do-do-do-do…
Do-do-do-do…

▶ 1:46/1:47 **Excuse Me, Please** [Unit 2]

(CHORUS)
Excuse me—please excuse me.
What's your number?
What's your name?
I would love to get to know you,
and I hope you feel the same.

I'll give you my e-mail address.
Write to me at my dot-com.
You can send a note in English
so I'll know
who it came from.
Excuse me—please excuse me.
Was that 0078?
Well, I think the class is starting,
and I don't
want to be late.

But it's really nice to meet you.
I'll be seeing you again.
Just call me on my cell phone
when you're looking for a friend.

(CHORUS)
So welcome to the classroom.
There's a seat right over there.
I'm sorry, but you're sitting in
our teacher's favorite chair!
Excuse me—please excuse me.
What's your number?
What's your name?

▶ 2:15/2:16 **Tell Me All About It** [Unit 4]

Tell me about your father.
He's a doctor and he's very tall.
And how about your mother?
She's a lawyer. That's her picture on
the wall.
Tell me about your brother.
He's an actor, and he's twenty-three.
And how about your sister?
She's an artist. Don't you think she looks
like me?

(CHORUS)
Tell me about your family—
who they are and what they do.
Tell me all about it.
It's so nice to talk with you.

Tell me about your family.
I have a brother and a sister, too.
And what about your parents?
Dad's a teacher, and my mother's eyes
are blue.

(CHORUS)
Who's the pretty girl in that photograph?
That one's me!
You look so cute!
Oh, that picture makes me laugh!
And who are the people there, right below
that one?
Let me see … that's my mom and dad.
They both look very young.

(CHORUS)
Tell me all about it.
Tell me all about it.

▶ 2:35/2:36 **Let's Make a Date** [Unit 5]

It's early in the evening—
6:15 P.M.
Here in New York City
a summer night begins.
I take the bus at seven
down the street from City Hall.
I walk around the corner
when I get your call.

(CHORUS)
Let's make a date.
Let's celebrate.
Let's have a great time out.

Let's meet in the Village
on Second Avenue
next to the museum there.
What time is good for you?
It's a quarter after seven.
There's a very good new show
weekdays at the theater.
Would you like to go?

(CHORUS)
Sounds great. What time's the show?
The first one is at eight.
And when's the second one?
The second show's too late.
OK, how do I get there?
The trains don't run at night.
No problem. Take a taxi.
The place is on the right.
Uh-oh! Are we late?
No, we're right on time.
It's 7:58.
Don't worry. We'll be fine!

(CHORUS)

▶ 3:15/3:16 **On the Weekend** [Unit 7]

(CHORUS)
On the weekend,
when we go out,
there is always so much joy and laughter.
On the weekend,
we never think about
the days that come before and after.

He gets up every morning.
Without warning, the bedside clock rings
the alarm.
So he gets dressed—
he does his best to be on time.
He combs his hair, goes down the stairs,
and makes some breakfast.
A bite to eat, and he feels fine.
Yes, he's on his way
to one more working day.

(CHORUS)
On Thursday night,
when he comes home from work,
he gets undressed, and if his room's a mess,
he cleans the house. Sometimes he takes
a rest.
Maybe he cooks something delicious,
and when he's done
he washes all the pots and dishes,
then goes to bed.
He knows the weekend's just ahead.

(CHORUS)

▶ 3:35/3:36 Home Is Where the Heart Is   [Unit 8]

There's a house for everyone
with a garden in the sun.
There's a stairway to the stars.
Where is this house?
It isn't far.

(CHORUS)
Home is where the heart is.
Home is where the heart is.

She lives on the second floor.
There are flowers at her front door.
There's a window with a breeze.
Love and kindness are the keys.

(CHORUS)

There's a room with a view of the sea.
Would you like to go there with me?

(CHORUS)

▶ 4:17/4:18 Fruit Salad, Baby   [Unit 10]

You never eat eggs for breakfast.
You don't drink coffee or tea.
I always end up cooking for you
when you're here with me.
I want to make something delicious,
'cause I like you a lot.
I'm checking my refrigerator,
and this is what I've got:

(CHORUS)
How about a fruit salad, baby—
apples, oranges, bananas too?
Well, here you go now, honey.
Good food coming up for me and you.

Are there any cans or bottles
or boxes on the shelf?
I put my dishes on the counter.
I mix everything well.

(CHORUS)

Chop and drain it.
Slice and dice it.
Mix and serve
with an ounce of love.
Pass your glass.
What are you drinking?
Tell me what dish
I am thinking of?

(CHORUS)

▶ 4:34/4:35 My Favorite Day   [Unit 11]

Last night we walked together.
It seems so long ago.
And we just talked and talked.
Where did the time go?
We saw the moonlit ocean
across the sandy beach.
The waves of summer fell,
barely out of reach.

(CHORUS)
Yes, that was then,
and this is now,
and all I do is think about
yesterday,
my favorite day of the week.

When I woke up this morning,
my feelings were so strong.
I put my pen to paper,
and I wrote this song.
I'm glad I got to know you.
You really made me smile.
My heart belonged to you
for a little while.

(CHORUS)

It was wonderful to be with you.
We had so much to say.
It was awful when we waved good-bye.
Why did it end that way?

(CHORUS)

▶ 5:17/5:18 She Can't Play Guitar   [Unit 13]

She can paint a pretty picture.
She can draw well every day.
She can dance and she can sing,
but she can't play guitar.
She can sew a dress so nicely,
and she does it beautifully.
She can knit a hundred sweaters,
but she can't play guitar.

(CHORUS)
And now it's too late.
She thinks it's too hard.
Her happy smile fades,
'cause she can't play guitar.

She can drive around the city.
She can fix a broken car.
She can be a great mechanic,
but she can't play guitar.

(CHORUS)
And she says,
"Could you please help me?
When did you learn?
Was it hard? Not at all?
Are my hands too small?"
She can cook a meal so nicely
in the kitchen, and there are
lots of things that she does well,
but she can't play guitar.

(CHORUS)

▶ 5:35/5:36 I Wasn't Born Yesterday   [Unit 14]

I went to school and learned the lessons
of the human heart.
I got an education in
psychology and art.
It doesn't matter what you say.
I know the silly games you play.

(CHORUS)
I wasn't born yesterday.
I wasn't born yesterday.

Well, pretty soon I graduated
with a good degree.
It took some time to understand
the way you treated me,
and it's too great a price to pay.
I've had enough, and anyway,

(CHORUS)

So you think I'd like to marry you
and be your pretty wife?
Well, that's too bad, I'm sorry, now.
Grow up and get a life!
It doesn't matter what you say.
I know the silly games you play.

(CHORUS)